FROM C
TO CROCՐDILES...

Answers to Questions

Answers to Questions

Also available:
From Beetroot to Buddhism...
From Comets to Cocaine...
From Elephants to Einstein...
From Limestone to Lucifer...
From Mammoths to Mediums...
From Sunspots to Strawberries...

FROM CRYSTALS TO CROCODILES...

Answers to Questions

RUDOLF STEINER

Ten discussions with workers at the Goetheanum in Dornach between 2 August and 30 September 1922

RUDOLF STEINER PRESS

Translation revised by Matthew Barton

Rudolf Steiner Press
Hillside House, The Square
Forest Row, East Sussex
RH18 5ES

www.rudolfsteinerpress.com

Published by Rudolf Steiner Press 2002
Previous English edition, translated by Joachim Reuter and revised by
Sabine H. Seiler, published under the title *The Human Being in Body, Soul
and Spirit* by Anthroposophic Press and Rudolf Steiner Press 1989

Originally published in German under the title *Die Erkenntnis des
Menschenwesens nach Leib, Seele und Geist, Über frühe Erdzustände* (volume
347 in the *Rudolf Steiner Gesamtausgabe* or Collected Works) by Rudolf
Steiner Verlag, Dornach. This authorized translation is based on the 3rd
edition, edited by Paul Gerhard Bellman, and is published by kind
permission of the Rudolf Steiner Nachlassverwaltung, Dornach. All
drawings in the text are by Leonore Uhlig and are based on Rudolf
Steiner's original blackboard drawings

A catalogue record for this book is available from the British Library

ISBN 1 85584 107 X

Cover by Andrew Morgan Design
Typeset by DP Photosetting, Aylesbury, Bucks.
Printed and bound in Great Britain by Cromwell Press Limited,
Trowbridge, Wilts.

Contents

Publisher's Foreword

The truly remarkable lectures—or, more accurately, question and answer sessions—contained in this book, form part of a series (published in eight volumes in the original German)* dating from August 1922 to September 1924. This series features talks given to people involved in various kinds of building work on Rudolf Steiner's architectural masterpieces, the first and second Goetheanums in Dornach, Switzerland. (The destruction by fire of the first Goetheanum necessitated the building of a replacement.) A vivid description of the different types of workers present, as well as the context and atmosphere of these talks, is given by a witness in the Appendix to the first volume of this English series, *From Elephants to Einstein* (1998).

The sessions arose out of explanatory tours of the Goetheanum which one of Steiner's pupils, Dr Roman Boos, had offered. When this came to an end, and the workers still wished to know more about the 'temple' they were involved with and the philosophy behind it, Dr Steiner agreed to take part in question and answer sessions himself. These took place during the working day, after the mid-morning break. Apart from the workmen, only a few other people were present: those working in the building office, and some of Steiner's closest colleagues. The subject-matter of the talks was chosen by the workers at the encouragement of Rudolf Steiner, who took their questions and usually gave immediate answers.

After Rudolf Steiner's death, some of the lectures—on the subject of bees—were published. However, as Marie Steiner

---

* 347–354 in the collected works of Rudolf Steiner, published by Rudolf Steiner Verlag, Dornach, Switzerland. For information on English translations, see the list on page xi.

writes in her original Preface to the German edition: 'Gradually more and more people felt a wish to study these lectures.' It was therefore decided to publish them in full. However, Marie Steiner's words about the nature of the lectures remain relevant to the present publication:

> They had, however, been intended for a particular group of people and Rudolf Steiner spoke off the cuff, in accord with the given situation and the mood of the workmen at the time. There was no intention to publish at the time. But the very way in which he spoke had a freshness and directness that one would not wish to destroy, for doing so would take away the special atmosphere that arose in the souls of those who asked the questions and him who gave the answers. It would be a pity to take away its special colour by pedantically rearranging sentences. We are therefore taking the risk of leaving them as far as possible untouched. This may not always accord with accustomed literary style, but on the other hand it preserves directness and vitality.

In this spirit, the translator has also been asked to preserve as much of the original style, or flavour, as possible. This might mean that readers need to study a passage several times, trying to bring to mind the live situation in which the talks were given, before the whole can be fully appreciated.

SG

Rudolf Steiner's Lectures to Workers at the Goetheanum

GA (*Gesamtausgabe*) number

347 *From Crystals to Crocodiles, Answers to Questions* (Rudolf Steiner Press 2002)

348 *From Comets to Cocaine, Answers to Questions* (Rudolf Steiner Press 2000)

349 *From Limestone to Lucifer, Answers to Questions* (Rudolf Steiner Press 1999)

350 *From Mammoths to Mediums, Answers to Questions* (Rudolf Steiner Press 2000)

351 Nine of the 15 lectures in the German edition are published in *Bees, Nine lectures on the Nature of Bees* (New York: Anthroposophic Press 1998)

352 *From Elephants to Einstein, Answers to Questions* (Rudolf Steiner Press 1998)

353 *From Beetroot to Buddhism, Answers to Questions* (Rudolf Steiner Press 1999)

354 *From Sunspots to Strawberries, Answers to Questions* (Rudolf Steiner Press 2002)

1. Discussion of 2 August 1922

On the origin of speech and languages

Good morning, gentlemen. Today we will add to what we have heard on previous occasions so that we will be better able to understand the full dignity of the human being.

I have explained roughly how nutrition and breathing work in human beings. We also talked about how closely connected nutrition is with our life and that it is essentially a process of taking in substances that then become lifeless in our intestines. These substances are then revitalized by the lymph vessels, and are transmitted into the blood as living substance. There this living nourishment encounters the air's oxygen. We take in air. The blood changes. This process occurs in the chest, and it is this process that gives us our feelings.

Thus life actually originates between the processes in the intestines and those in the blood. In turn, in the blood processes, that is, between the activities of the blood and the air, our feelings come about. Now we have to deal with the human mind as well and try to understand how it developed.

You see, understanding the external aspect of the mind has become possible only in the last 60 years. Last year, in 1921, we could have celebrated the sixtieth anniversary of this possibility. We did not, because in our time people are not very interested in celebrating purely scientific anniversaries. The discovery made in 1861 which we could have celebrated 60 years later, was an important scientific discovery. It is only in the last 50 or 60 years that one can speak about the things I wish to mention today. I remember it because it is just as old as I am. The discovery I am speaking of is the following.

I told you the other day how we can observe human beings. We do not need to experiment; all we need to do is pay attention to how nature itself experiments with people whenever they have any kind of illness. If we know how to look at what happens to the physical body when a person becomes ill in any way, we discover that nature itself arranged such an experiment for us and that we can gain insights from it.

Well, in 1861, when Broca dissected brains of deceased people who had speech impairments, he discovered that they had an injury in the third convolution on the left side of the brain.[1]

You know, don't you, that when we remove the top of the skull, we can see the brain? This brain has convolutions. We call one of them the temple convolution because it is located near the temple. Well now, in every person suffering from speech impediments or muteness, there is some damage in this left convolution of the brain. This injury happens when someone has a so-called stroke. What happens in that case? The blood, which normally flows only through the vessels, is forced out through their walls and enters the tissue surrounding the vessels, where it should not be. Such a haemorrhage produces the stroke, the paralysis. In other words, whenever blood flows into the wrong place, into this convolution of the brain, it ultimately disables this temple convolution completely and prevents the person from speaking.

This is an interesting connection: human beings can speak because they have a healthy left convolution of the brain. We must now understand what it means when a person has a healthy left convolution of the brain. But in order to grasp this, we need to look at something else first.

When we examine this same area of the brain in small children who have died, we find that this portion constitutes a fairly uniform, mushlike substance, especially at the time before the child has learned to speak. As the infant gradually learns to speak, more and more small whorls develop here. They continue to form in an artful way. In other words, the left cerebral convolutions in the child who has learned to speak or in a fully grown adult are artfully structured.

Clearly, this means that something happened to the brain while the child learned to speak. And we should not think about this any differently than we think in ordinary life. You see, if I move a table from there to here, nobody would say the table moved itself this way. It would be just as wrong for me to say that the brain has formed these convolutions by itself. Instead, I must think about what has actually taken place and what caused it. In other words, I must ask why the left temple convolution developed this way.

You see, when children learn to speak, they move their body. In particular, they move their speech organs. Before that, when they could not yet talk, they were merely fidgety, cried, and so forth. As long as the child is only able to cry, its left convolution of the brain is still a 'mush', as I described it. The more the child learns not merely to cry but also to turn this crying into individual sounds, the more this convolution receives definite shape. As long as the infant simply cries, there is only brain mush in this area. When the child begins to utter sounds, this uniform mush is transformed into the artfully structured left portion of the brain we can see in healthy adults.

Now, gentlemen, the matter is like this: When children cry, the sounds they utter are mainly vowels such as A [as in 'father'] or E [as in 'met']. When they merely cry like this, they do not need a developed left cerebral convolution; the children utter these sounds out of themselves, without having anything artful developed in the brain. If we pay some attention, we will discover that children initially make

Ah sounds; later on they add those of *U* [as in 'shoe'] and *EE* ['bee']. Gradually, as you know, they also learn to utter consonants. First they form the sound *Ah*; then they add *M* or *W* and say *MA* or *WA*. In other words, out of their crying children gradually manage to form words by adding consonants to the vowels.

And how do they form these consonants? All you need to do is pay attention to how you pronounce, for example, an *M*. You'll see that you must move your lips. When you were a child, you had to learn this through imitation. If you say *L*, you must move your tongue. Thus you must always move some organs. From aimless movements the child must progress to regular movements, carried out by the speech organs in imitation. The more the child moves beyond the vowels formed in mere crying and utters consonants such as *L, M, N, R*, the more the left cerebral convolution is structured in an artful way.

Now we could ask how children initially learn to speak. They learn to speak only through imitation. They learn to speak, to move their lips, by imitating out of their feelings the way other people move their lips. All of this is imitation. This means that children take in, see, perceive what happens around them. And this perceiving, this mental activity, forms the brain. Just as a carver shapes a piece of wood or a sculptor works on marble and bronze, so the child's movements 'sculpt' the brain. The organs the child moves carry their movements right into the brain.

If I want to pronounce *L*, I have to use my tongue. The tongue is connected with the brain through nerves and through other organs. This *L* penetrates into my left cerebral convolution and produces a structure there. In other words, the *L* produces forms in which one section joins the next, almost resembling something like the intestines. The *M* produces spherical convolutions. So you see, these sounds work on the brain.

The movements of the organs the child activates through observation are at work here in the brain. It is very interesting that since it became known that a brain stroke damages the left cerebral convolution, thus destroying the ability to speak, it became possible to know that the formation of vowels and consonants by the child continuously works on this convolution. This in turn is based on the fact that the eyes and other sense organs perceive what takes place in the world around us. And what happens in the world around us? Well, you see, whenever we speak, we are also breathing. We breathe continuously. And in this process, every breath first enters the human body, moves up the spinal column and enters the brain. This means that even while the child is crying— though as yet unable to pronounce consonants—this breath moves up and enters the brain.

What is actually entering the brain in this process? Well, blood, of course. As I explained to you in the last few days, blood flows everywhere. Through our breathing, blood is constantly being pushed into the brain. This activity begins the very moment we are born and even before, except then it occurs in a different manner. Anyhow, when we are born, we begin to breathe. This intake of air begins, which then pushes blood into the brain.

Thus we can say that as long as the baby's breathing merely pushes blood into the brain, it can only cry. Children begin to speak when not only blood is forced into the brain, but when they also perceive something through their eyes or any other organ, especially the ears. In other words, whenever they see another person move, children inwardly repeat this movement. At this moment not only the bloodstream goes up to the head, but another stream goes there as well, for instance from the ears—the stream of the nerves.

In the left cerebral convolution, like everywhere else in the human body, blood vessels and nerve fibres meet. The latter are affected by what we observe and perceive. The child's movements in uttering consonants reach the left convolution, that of speech, via the nerves. This area is structured by the combined effect of the breathing, which is carried there by the blood, and of whatever activity comes in through the ears and the eyes. In other words, blood and nerves together structure this brain mush beautifully. Thus we see that, at least in this particular region (and in fact the same thing occurs in other parts too), our brain is actually structured through the combined activity of perception (via the nerves) and of the constant intake of breath, which pushes the blood into the brain.

At this point, we also need to understand that this is how the child learns to speak, that is, by developing the left cerebral convolution. But, gentlemen, when you dissect a corpse, you will find that the right convolution of the brain, though symmetrically placed, shows relatively little structuring. On the one hand we have the left convolution, which is beautifully formed as I said before. On the other we have the right one, which throughout life usually remains the way it was in the young child, that is, unstructured. You can say that if we had only the right convolution we would only be able to cry. It is only because we so artfully structure the left convolution that we are able to speak.

You see, it is only when a person is left-handed and habitually tends to do most of his work with the left hand that, strangely enough, he will not lose his capacity for speech even when his left side is affected by a stroke. Dissection will reveal that in the case of this left-handed person, the right convolution of the brain was structured in the same way as the left convolution of right-handed people normally is. Movements of arms and hands, then, have a strong bearing on the formation of the brain.

Why is that so? You see, this comes about because when a person is used to doing a lot of things with his right hand, he does not merely do them with this hand, but he also gets into the habit of breathing a bit more strongly on the right side, of exerting more of an effort there. He also gets into the habit of hearing more clearly on the right side, and so forth. All of this merely points to the fact that the person in the habit of using his right hand develops the tendency to be more active on that side than on the left.

When a person is right-handed, the left convolution of the brain is structured; when he is left-handed, the right convolution is structured. What is the reason for this? Well, gentlemen, when you look at the right arm and hand and the head and the left cerebral convolution and then examine where the nerves are, you will find that there are nerves everywhere in the human body. If you did not have nerves everywhere, you could not feel warm or cold. These sensations have to do with the nerves. You have nerves everywhere in your body. They go up the spine and reach right into the brain. But the remarkable thing is that the nerves coming from the right hand lead into the left portion of the brain, and the ones in the other hand are connected with the right side of the brain. This is because the nerves cross. Yes, the nerves cross in the brain. For instance, if I do a gymnastics exercise or a eurythmic movement with my right hand or the right arm, I sense the activity through this nerve, but I become aware of it in the left half of the brain because the nerves cross.

Let us now imagine that a child prefers to do everything with the right hand. Then the child will also breathe a bit more strongly on the right side and will also hear and see a bit better on that side. The person will make greater efforts on that side and through his movements develop something that reaches into the left side of the brain. Now you only need to imagine that we have the habit of making certain gestures while speaking, such as *Ah! [corresponding gesture]*; or if we reject something: *Eh!* These gestures are sensed by our nerves. Now, the movements we make with the right hand while speaking are experienced by the left side of the brain.

By the same token, those of us who are right-handed tend to pronounce vowels and consonants more strongly with the right half of the larynx. Again these activities are taken in more vividly with the left side of the brain. This is why the brain, originally more like mush, is now a lot more structured. In contrast, we use the left side of our body much less, and that is why the right half of the brain is less developed and remains unformed. However, when someone is left-handed, the opposite process takes place.

These facts lead to important conclusions for education. Just think, when you have left-handed children (you will have a few of them), you must tell yourself that whereas all the others have a very artfully developed left convolution of the brain, in the left-handed children the right convolution is structured. When I teach writing, I use my right hand. In this activity, the right-handed children will merely reinforce what they have begun to develop in their left brain convolution when they began learning to speak. However, if I now force the left-handed children to write with their right hand, I will destroy the development that learning to speak has produced in their right cerebral convolution. Yes, this development will be destroyed.

Since left-handed children are not supposed to write with their left hand, my task is now to gradually direct everything previously carried out by the left hand to the right one. This way they will initially learn to do simple things with the right hand and get into writing much more slowly than the other children. But it does not matter if they learn to write a bit later. If I simply were to make left-handed children write as fast as the right-handed ones, I would make them less intelligent because I would ruin the development that has taken place in the right side of the brain. Therefore I must make sure to treat left-handed children differently from right-handed ones when I teach them to write. This approach will not make them less intelligent in later life, but more so, because I gradually transform their left-handedness into right-handedness, instead of merely getting their entire brain confused through making them write with the right hand immediately. If you want to affect the entire human being through writing and force this change to the right hand, pedagogically speaking you would achieve the very opposite of what you are striving for.

Nowadays we find a widespread tendency to teach people to do everything with both hands. This is how we really get their brains mixed up. This tendency of making people do the same thing both with the right and the left hand merely proves how little we know. Mind you, we can strive for such an ideal, but before we could realize it, we would have to change something. Gentlemen, we would first have to change the entire human being! We would slowly have to shift activities from the left side to the right and then gradually weaken them on the right. What would happen then? You see, what would happen is that, below the surface, the left cerebral convolution would be more artfully formed; but on the outside, it would remain mush. The same would happen to the right convolution. Instead of distributing two activities between the left and the right sides, we would develop each convolution into an outer and an inner half.

The inner portion would be more suitable for speech; the outer one would exist merely in order to add the vowels and consonants in crying. However, speech is a combination of what happens in crying and in articulating. This remains the same throughout life.

You see, we cannot just tinker with human beings and their development. In education, even in the lower grades, we need an understanding of the entire human being. For with everything we do we change the human being. The really criminal thing is that nowadays people just tinker with things externally and ignore the inner effects of what they do. Actually, very few people have both sides of the brain fully developed. Usually the right convolution contains more blood vessels, whereas the left one has fewer and instead is more permeated with nerves. This holds true for the human brain generally; the right side carries more blood, and the left is more used for perceiving.

Once we realize that the brain is shaped under external influences, we can appreciate how important these influences from the outside world are. We see that they are tremendously significant once we understand that they affect everything that takes place in the brain. Also, by understanding what occurs in the brain when we speak, we can get an idea of how the human brain works.

You see, when we examine it further, we discover that there are always more blood vessels on the outside wall of the brain than inside it. Thus we can say that the exterior part of the brain contains more blood and the interior more nerves.

Let us now consider a child learning to speak in the ordinary way, a right-handed child. How is the brain of such a child being formed? First of all, the brain of a young child is surrounded by a layer or mantle, so to speak, of blood vessels. Then nerve tracts begin to form. Because of this, gentlemen, because of these nerve tracts in there, the inner brain substance appears whitish when you take it out and look at it. However, when you take out the brain matter surrounding it, it looks reddish-grey because it contains so many blood vessels.

Now what happens in this region when the child learns to speak and consequently the left cerebral convolution is structured accordingly? What takes place, you see, is that the nerve bundles, as it were, gradually extend more towards the inside and less in the area where the blood system expands. In other words, in children who develop normally the inner part of the brain shifts more to the left and the remaining portion follows. The brain thus moves to the left side, where it turns ever more whitish. It shifts that way. All of human development is based on such artful details.

Now let us talk some more about speech. You see, there are languages that have many consonants and others that contain many vowels such as *A, E, I* and so forth. In some languages people squeeze out the sounds, like *S, W,* so that one barely hears the vowels. What lies behind all this?

We know that languages differ in different regions of the earth. What does it mean when someone lives in a certain area where people focus more on the consonants? It means that he or she experiences the outer world more, for the consonants are formed through the experience of outer surroundings. Therefore, in people living more in the physical world the white portion of the brain shifts more to the left. In people experiencing life more inwardly, people living in a region where things are experienced more inwardly, the white brain matter does not move quite so far to the left. These people will tend to utter melodious vowels. This varies with the regions of the earth.

Let us now assume the following, gentlemen: let's imagine the earth and people standing at various points on the earth. And one person, let us say, is given a language rich in vowels and another one a language rich in consonants. What must have happened in their respective regions? A lot may have happened, quite a lot, but I want to focus on one thing that may have taken place. Imagine that we have high mountains and a level area, a plain. Picture then steep mountains on one side and a plain on the other. Now, wherever there are flat regions, we perceive that the language people speak there is richer in vowels. Wherever there are steep mountains, the local language tends to be richer in consonants.

But you see, this matter is not so simple after all, because we must ask how the mountains and the plains came about. This is the way it is. We have the earth, and the sun shines upon it. At one time our entire earth was unformed mush. The mountains first had to be pulled out of this mush. The earth was basically mush and the mountains were pulled up out of it.

Well, gentlemen, what was it that pulled the mountains up? The cosmic forces that work out there did. We can say that there are certain forces of a cosmic nature that pulled up these mountains. In some places the forces were strong and developed mountains; in other places there were weaker forces coming in out of the surrounding cosmos that did not produce mountains. In this latter area the earth crust was not pulled up so strongly in primeval times. And the people born on those parts of the earth's crust less affected by these cosmic forces use more vowels. Persons born in areas more strongly influenced by the cosmic forces use more consonants. We see now that the differences between languages are connected with the forces of the entire universe.

Now how can we support such a claim? Well, gentlemen, what we have claimed here must be considered in the same way we look at clocks to check the time. We look at the clock to see if we must start working or if it is time to leave. But we never say, 'This won't do! This awful minute hand is a terrible fellow who whips me on to work.' We wouldn't dream of saying that. All the clock does is tell us when we have to go to work, and so we cannot blame it for having to work, can we? In this case, the clock is completely innocent.

Similarly, we can look up to the sun and say that when we

stand here at a certain moment, the sun is between us and the constellation of Aries. That is the direction where these strong cosmic forces work from. It is not Aries itself, of course. This constellation merely indicates the direction where the strong forces come from. If a person is standing in a different place at that same time, he or she is affected as follows: when the sun has moved to that place, it is in Virgo, let us say. The forces coming from this direction are weaker. Instead of going through the entire process now, I can therefore say that when someone is born in an area where at a certain time, let's say at his birth, the sun is in Aries, that person will tend to use more consonants. However, when someone is born with the sun in Virgo, he will tend to use more vowels.

You see, I can read the entire zodiac like a clock from which I can see what happens on earth. But I must always keep in mind that it is not the constellations that cause these events; they are only indicators. From this you can see that the zodiac can tell us a lot, even about the reasons why languages on earth differ.

Now, let us look at the earth and imagine that we put a chair out into space and look back at the earth. Of course, this is only possible in our imagination and not in reality. When we look from our chair in space at the various languages on earth, as in a sort of language map, then we get a certain picture. When we then turn the chair around and look out into the universe, we get a picture of the stars. And the two pictures match.

If we study the Southern Hemisphere and the languages there and then turn the chair around and examine the southern firmament, our experience is entirely different from the one we would have if we did the same thing in the Northern Hemisphere. This means that we could draw a map of the starry skies above us, and from our study of the connection between the stars and language we would then be able to tell which language is spoken under a particular constellation.

You see now that as soon as we begin to observe human spiritual life, for example the formation of our minds through speech, we must look up to the stars in order to understand anything. The earth alone does not give us an answer; you can think about why languages are different as long as you like, but based on the earth alone you won't find an explanation.

If you want to know what takes place in your stomach, you must examine the earth, the soil below. If a region grows mainly cabbages, you will understand that people there must constantly revitalize in their metabolism the heads of cabbage pulled out of the soil. In other words, if you want to know what people in a certain area eat, you must examine the soil. If you are interested in how people breathe in a particular region, you have to study the atmosphere. And if you want to know what happens inside the skull, in this brain of ours, you must look at the position of the stars. You always have to see the human being as an integrated part of the entire universe.

You see now that it is indeed mere superstition to say, 'Whenever the sun is in Aries, such and such takes place.' This kind of statement is worthless. However, if you understand the full context, the matter ceases to be superstition and becomes science instead. And that will lead us from understanding the transformation of substances to an understanding of what is really happening and its connection to the vast universe out there.

2. Discussion of 5 August 1922

On the human etheric body. Relationships between brain and thinking

Good morning, gentlemen. I would like to continue today with yesterday's subject. After all, we can fully understand a subject only if we deal with it in more and more depth.

As we saw last time, an important fact concerning human beings is that they take in nourishment from the earth, and air from the atmosphere surrounding the earth. It is really only because of this that human beings live and develop into feeling and sentient beings. As we saw, they take in forces from the whole cosmos, and it is only through this that human beings can think and thus become truly human.

In other words, we must be able to feed ourselves and to breathe in order to become sentient beings. We must also be able to absorb forces out of the entire universe in order to become thinking beings. We can no more become thinking beings by ourselves than we can learn to speak all by ourselves. Human beings can no more think out of themselves than they can feed on themselves.

Let us now look more closely at how these things work. First, let's try to understand the process of nutrition. We take in food that reaches our intestines in a lifeless condition. The lymph glands re-enliven it and the lymph carries it into our blood, which is constantly renewed through our breathing. The blood, or actually the force of the blood, that is the breath, travels along the spinal cord and rises into the brain, where it connects itself with the activity of the brain.

You need only look at how the nutrition of children differs from that of adults, and you will be able to understand much about the nature of the human being. As you know, children must drink a lot of milk in the first years of life. In the beginning, they take in nothing but milk. What are the implications of the fact that babies are fed only milk? We can grasp the significance of this only when we understand what milk consists of.

We are usually not aware that milk is 87 per cent water. In other words, when we drank milk as infants, 87 per cent of what we took in was water and only the remaining 13 per cent was something else. Of the remaining 13 per cent only 4.5 per cent is protein; another 4 per cent is fat, and the rest consists of minerals and so on. Basically, what babies take in when they drink milk is water.

As I told you earlier, human beings consist essentially of liquids. In children, the quantities of these liquids must constantly be increased. Children must grow and therefore require a lot of water, which they take in with their milk.

At this point you may say that we might as well give babies only those 13 per cent that are nutritious and for the balance just offer them water to drink. Well, you see, the human body is not equipped for that. What we get with milk is not just 13 per cent of ordinary protein, fat and so on, but all these substances are dissolved in the milk, are dissolved in the water contained in milk. When infants drink milk, they take in the substances they need in a dissolved state. This means that the child's body does not have to do the work of dissolving the fat, protein, and so on.

Remember what I said earlier about nutrition: all the food substances we eat must first be dissolved in the mouth. In a way, nature allows us to take in solid food only as far as our mouths. There we have to dissolve it with our own fluids. The other digestive organs, such as stomach, intestines, and so forth, can only use dissolved substances. Children must first acquire this ability to dissolve solid matter. At first, they cannot do it alone. Therefore, they must receive food that is already dissolved. You can tell how important this is when you consider that infants brought up on synthetic food preparations will be stunted in their growth.

Now you may wonder if it is possible to produce artificial milk, that is, if we dissolved the 13 per cent solids, such as protein, fat and so on, in water so that the solution would look like milk, would it be equivalent to the milk children normally receive? You see, gentlemen, it would not be equivalent. If an infant were given such artificial milk, its development would be stunted. And since people produce only what is needed, one would have to give up the production of such milk. This synthetic milk would be harmful.

What is it that alone can bring about this dissolving of substance that the child needs? Only life itself can do it. The animals can do it to an extent, but not all of them. At the beginning of life, babies cannot dissolve protein, fat, and so forth. They depend on having these substances dissolved for them in the proper way. Thus they actually receive proper nourishment only through mother's milk.

Of all animal milk, that of the donkey most closely resembles human milk. When an infant cannot be breast-fed, it can be fed with donkey's milk. This may appear strange; however, the fact is donkey's milk most closely resembles human milk, and in the absence of the latter one can keep a donkey mare in a stable and thus supply the infant with milk. Of course, I mention this only as a hypothetical situation in order to illustrate how things are connected in nature.

For instance, if you compare the nutritional value of milk with that of a chicken egg, you find that the egg contains approximately 14 per cent protein. That's a lot more than we find in milk, actually four times as much. By the time children are fed such solid foods that contain more protein, they must have developed the capacity to dissolve solid substances on their own.

From these facts you can see how important it is that

children get liquid nourishment. But what kind of liquid food? Food that has been filled with life and that, if possible, still contains life forces. This is provided only through breast-feeding by the mother.

When infants drink milk, it passes through mouth and oesophagus into the stomach. In this process, the milk loses its life; it is killed, so to speak, but it is then re-enlivened in the intestines. Thus we see already in children that life must first be destroyed. Since the living food has undergone only little change, infants need to exert less digestive effort for re-enlivening milk than for any other food.

This also shows us something else. If we think about this matter in the right way, what do we notice? Let us think in the right way here. As we said, infants must take in living nourishment, which is first destroyed and then re-en-livened. Now, human beings consist largely of liquids, but can we therefore say that they consist of water, the water we find in lifeless nature? If this were so, the water we find in lifeless nature around us should be able to work in children in the same way it works in adults, who, after all, have gathered more life forces. Here we see that the almost 90 per cent water we have in our bodies is not the ordinary, lifeless water we find in nature; it is a different, an enlivened substance. In other words, what we have in our bodies is a unique fluid: it is enlivened water. It is like the water we find in lifeless nature but filled with the life forces that penetrate the entire world. However, these forces are as little active in the lifeless water in nature as thinking is in a corpse. Therefore, when you speak of water in a creek and water in the human body, you will understand the differ-ence between them if you think of the water in the creek as the corpse of the water that is in the human body.

Thus we can say that in our bodies we have not only lifeless, physical matter but also a life body. This is where correct thinking will lead us, to the insight that every human being has a life organism, a life body. When we study the relationship of the human being to nature, we can see how this organism functions within us. We must first study nature and then look at the human being. When we study nature, we find just about everywhere all the substances we have in our bodies. The only difference is that we have processed these natural substances in our own particular ways.

We'll understand this better if we study the smallest creatures, one-celled organisms. As I describe them, you will see that I am speaking of these smallest and least developed creatures in nature in the same way I spoke of what is inside the human being. You see, in the ocean there are very small creatures. They are actually nothing but small gelatinous lumps, so small that one can see them only with a strong magnifying glass. I will draw them for you, enlarged of course [*see drawing below, left part*]. These tiny gelatinous lumps float in the water.

If there were nothing but these small lumps and the surrounding water, they would be at rest. But if a small grain of some substance approaches [*see drawing above, right part*] this creature expands its gelatinous substance until its body fluid envelops the grain. Of course, when it expands its substance, the little lump moves in the direction of the grain. This is how the small lump moves. In other words, by the very act of enveloping a tiny grain of another substance with its own body substance this tiny creature moves. Then it will begin to dissolve the grain inside its body. Thus, this one-celled creature has eaten the grain.

These organisms can of course eat several such tiny grains. Imagine we saw a creature here and a grain there, and there another one and over there two more [*see drawing below*]. The tiny organism will now stretch its feelers this way and that way. The direction in which it extends most, where it encounters the largest grain, that is the direction in which it will move, pulling the other extensions along. This organism moves by feeding at the same time.

Well, gentlemen, when I describe how these small gelatinous lumps move around in the ocean and feed at the same time, you will remember my description of the so-called white blood cells in human beings. At first glance we realize that they do the same thing inside us; they float in our blood, moving along while they feed, just like those small lumps I described. We understand what it is that moves around in our blood when we look at the one-celled creatures that float in the ocean. We bear such creatures within us.

Having understood that in a certain sense we have the same organisms floating around in our blood that we find outside in nature, let us now look at the nervous system, particularly the brain. The brain also consists of very small particles. When I draw these smallest parts, we realize that they, too, consist of some kind of lumpy, thick, and slimy substance. Several extensions consisting of the same substance radiate outward from this slimelike matter [*see drawing below*]. When we look at such a brain cell, we see that it stretches out its tiny feet or arms and touches those of the neighbouring cells. These cells can be very long; some extend almost through half the body, and each one of them is again located next to others. When we study the human brain under a microscope, it appears like a number of dots in which the slimelike substance is more densely concentrated. Thick branches extend from there and intertwine. If you imagine a dense forest with thick tree crowns and big, interweaving branches, you get an idea of what the human brain looks like under a microscope.

Now you may say, all right, we have just heard a description of these white corpuscles living in our blood. The brain has been described as very similar; it, too, consists of many particles such as those we find in the blood. Thus, if we could remove all the white corpuscles from the blood without killing the person, and if we could put them neatly into the brain, after having removed that also, then we would have created a brain for that individual out of his or her own white blood cells.

However, the strange thing is that before we could create a brain out of these white corpuscles, they would have to be almost dead. This is the difference between the white blood cells and the brain cells. The white corpuscles are full of life; they move around in our blood. I told you that they surge through the blood vessels just like the blood itself. Then they leave their original habitat. As I mentioned earlier, they become gourmets and even move all the way to the surface of the body. They move around everywhere in the human body.

In contrast to those cells, you will find that the brain cells always stay in one place. They are at rest. Each one merely extends its branches and thus touches the nearest neighbour. Whereas the white corpuscles are in constant motion, the brain cells are at rest and in fact are almost dead.

Let us think once more of that tiny organism floating in the ocean. Let's imagine that one day it eats too much. It extends its arm, takes in food here and there, and overeats. This is more than the small creature can take, and so it divides; it splits into two. Instead of one organism there are now two. The original one has multiplied. Our white corpuscles also have the ability to multiply. There are always some dying off and others being produced in this way.

The brain cells, which I drew for you, cannot multiply. The white blood cells are full of life, independent life, and they can reproduce. However, the intertwining brain cells cannot reproduce. One brain cell will never turn into two. As the brain grows and increases in size, new, additional cells must move into the brain from the rest of the body. They must grow into the brain. The cells in the brain never multiply there, but merely accumulate. As long as we grow, new cells must constantly move into our head from the rest of the body, so that we have a sufficiently large brain when we are grown up.

The fact that the brain cells cannot multiply already tells us that they are almost dead. They are constantly in the process of dying. When we think about this in the right way, we discover a marvellous contrast in the human being. In the blood, we have cells, the white corpuscles, that are full of life, of a desire to live. In the brain, on the other hand, we have cells that actually have a constant wish to die, that are constantly in the process of dying. Thus it is true that as far as the brain is concerned human beings are in a constant process of dying. The brain is constantly on the verge of dying.

Well, gentlemen, I am sure you have heard of people who fainted, or perhaps you have experienced this yourselves. I know it is an embarrassing thing to experience. When people faint, they feel like they are falling. They lose consciousness.

What has actually taken place in a person who loses consciousness this way? You know, I am sure, that very pale persons, such as anaemic girls, faint very easily. Why is that so? Well, you see, they faint because in proportion to the red corpuscles, they have too many white ones. Human beings must have a certain proportion of white to red corpuscles to be properly conscious. What then does it mean to lose consciousness, for example, in fainting or in sleeping? It means that the white corpuscles are too active. When this happens, we have, as it were, too much life in us, and as a result we lose consciousness. Therefore it is very good that we have cells in our head that have a constant desire to die. If these white corpuscles in our brain, too, were to be very much alive, we would not have any consciousness at all, but would always be asleep.

Now you may want to ask why plants are always asleep? Well, this is because they don't have such living organisms within them. Actually, they have no blood at all and therefore do not have this independent life that we bear within us.

If we want to compare the human brain with something similar in nature, we must look at plants. In fact our brain constantly undermines the life we have within us, thus creating consciousness. Our understanding of the brain leads to a paradox. There is indeed a contradiction in the fact that the plant has no consciousness, but human beings do. This is something we can explain only after long and careful thinking, which we will begin now.

As you know, we lose consciousness every night, when we sleep. Clearly, something is going on there in our body that we must now try to comprehend. You see, gentlemen, if the same processes were taking place in the body when we sleep as in the waking state, we would not be able to sleep. When we sleep, our brain cells begin to be a bit more alive than when we are awake. In other words, they then begin to more closely resemble those cells that have an independent life inside us. Picture it like this: when we are awake, our brain cells are completely at rest; when we are asleep, they still cannot move around, because they are held in place, and cannot float around, for they would immediately come up against obstacles. Yet one could say that they now summon up the will to move. The brain thus becomes restless. Because of this inner restlessness of the brain we become unconscious when we sleep.

Now we must ask how human thinking originates. How is it that we are able to take in forces out of the entire universe? With our digestive organs we can absorb only earth forces in the various substances we take in. With our respiratory organs we can absorb only the air, in the form of oxygen. In order to take in all the forces of the entire universe, the head must be at rest. The brain must be completely at rest. But when we sleep the brain begins to be restless; then we take in fewer forces from the universe and lose consciousness.

But there is more to it than this. Let's assume some work is being done at two different places. For instance, here it is done by two men and over there by five. The parts they produce are then assembled later. At a certain point it becomes necessary to reduce the amount of work in one place because too much was produced there, and in the other place not enough parts were made. What do we usually do in such a case? We ask one of the five workers to join the other two. Then we have three workers at one site and only four at the other. Thus we shift some of the work around if we don't want to increase the output.

Similarly, human beings have only a limited amount of forces or energy at their disposal, and they must distribute them carefully. The strength required to increase the brain activity when we sleep must be withdrawn from other areas of the body. Where is it drawn from? It is withdrawn from some of the white blood cells. Some of them are less active when we sleep. The brain becomes more active when we are asleep, while some of the white blood cells become less lively. This is the compensation I spoke about before.

Remember, I also said that because the brain is less alive and comes to rest, human beings are able to think. Since the white corpuscles are more at rest during the night, we should actually begin to think. We should be able to think with our bodies.

Is it possible that human beings think at night with their bodies? That's a tricky question, isn't it? All we can say at first is that we are certainly not aware of it. However, that we are not aware of something does not necessarily prove that it doesn't exist. If it did, then everything we have not yet seen would also not exist. Indeed, the human body may think at night for all we know; since we are not aware of it, we would have to deny it.

Now let's see if there are any clues indicating that while we think with our heads during the day we may actually think at night with the liver, the stomach, and the other organs, perhaps even with the intestines. In all of us there are certain indications that this is indeed so. Just think how it is possible that something exists even though we are not aware of it. For instance, while standing here and talking to you, I focus my attention on you, and that means that I am not aware of what is going on behind my back.

This can lead to strange incidents. For example, during these lectures, I may be in the habit of occasionally sitting down on this chair. While I focus my attention on you, someone removes the chair. I cannot see it happen, but happen it did. I will certainly become aware of the effects as soon as I try to sit down! You see, we must judge things not only on the basis of what we normally know, but also on the basis of what we may know indirectly. If I had just happened to look back quickly, I would probably not have sat on the floor. If I had taken a look, I would have avoided doing that.

Let us study thinking as it occurs in the human body. You see, scientists love to talk about the limitations of human cognition. What do they mean by that? They mean that whatever they have not yet seen — with the naked eye, the telescope, or the microscope — does not exist. But to suppose this is like continually sitting on the floor by mistake — for not seeing something happen does not mean it hasn't.

In order to become aware of something, I must not only think about it but also observe what I have thought of. The thinking going on in me may be a continuous process, sometimes occurring in the head and at other times in the entire body. But when I am awake, I have my eyes open. The eyes do not only look outwards, but also perceive inwardly. Similarly, we do not only taste food in the mouth, but also perceive inwardly that, for instance, the body as a whole is ill and therefore something otherwise delicious is now disgusting to us. In fact, this inner aspect is always the determining factor. This perception of what goes on inside us is as essential as the perception of what is outside us.

Imagine you wake up as usual. Your brain cells gradually slow down their activity and come to rest, and you can begin to use your senses again. This normal way of waking up, completely in accordance with the normal rhythm in life, is one way of waking up. However, it is also possible that for some reason your brain cells come to rest too abruptly. Then something else happens. Going back to the example of the workers, let us imagine that the person in charge of a project sends the fifth worker from one site to join the other crew. Under certain conditions, this may work out very smoothly. However, let's assume that there are two foremen. One of them must remove a worker from the one site and the other one must put him to work at the second site. This may not work out so smoothly, especially if the two supervisors argue about whether or not this is a good idea. Similarly, if the brain cells come to rest abruptly, the white corpuscles which were inactive during sleep may not be able to function again so quickly. So it may happen that while the brain cells are already at rest again the white blood cells are not yet ready to get up. They insist on getting some more rest and will not get up.

It would be marvellous if we could directly perceive these lazy blood corpuscles that, figuratively speaking, want to stay in bed. We would then look at them as we normally look at the brain cells and perceive the most wonderful thoughts in them. At the very moment when we wake up too abruptly, we would then perceive the most marvellous thoughts. We can understand this easily, gentlemen, if we look at the connection between the human being and nature. If nothing else interfered and we woke up abruptly, we would perceive the most marvellous thoughts in our body. However, we can't do that. Why is this so? You see, between these lazy, sleepy white blood cells and the perceiving organs in the head occurs the entire process of breathing, which involves the red corpuscles. Breathing is a continuous process, and we must therefore study the thinking processes in the whole breathing process.

Imagine you are waking up and your brain comes to rest. In your blood there float some white corpuscles. If you could perceive them when they are at rest, you would see the most beautiful thoughts in them. However the entire breathing process is also mixed up in this. This is as though you were looking at something through a cloudy piece of glass; everything will be blurred and nebulous. The breathing process is like the cloudy piece of glass; it blurs the thinking going on in the body below the head. This is what then gives rise to dreams. Dreams originate from the vague thoughts we perceive when the nightly activity of the brain cells comes to rest too abruptly.

Something similar happens sometimes when we fall asleep. The brain may become active too slowly and still have the ability to perceive something when thinking in the body is already beginning. Then we can observe this thinking as we fall asleep. We are not aware of these inner thoughts for most of the night, during deep sleep, but while we are falling asleep or waking up, we can perceive them in the form of dreams. And we actually become aware of dreams only at the moment of waking up, as you will see when you study a dream carefully.

For example, let's say you are sleeping, and there is a

chair next to your bed. Now you dream that you are a student at a university and one day you meet another student. There is an exchange of angry words, and you insult him. He cannot ignore the insult and must react, and challenges you to a duel.[1] Well, you dream all the other details. The two of you select seconds and walk out into the woods. Then you start shooting; there is the first shot. You hear it in your dream and wake up. Then you realize that you merely knocked over the chair by your bed. That was the shot you heard!

Well, gentlemen, the entire dream would not have occurred if you had not knocked over the chair. The dream developed as it did only at the moment of waking up, for after all it was the falling chair that woke you up. In other words this picture, the blurring of what was going on inside you, came about only at the moment of waking up. This shows you that the pictorial element of dreams can only be formed at precisely the moment of waking up or falling asleep.

When we form such pictures and can perceive something in them, we must also have thoughts about them. Where does this insight lead us? It brings us to some understanding of sleeping and waking. Let us ask then what sleeping really means. When we sleep, the brain is more active than when we are awake, and it comes to rest when we are awake. You see, gentlemen, if we were to say that the brain is more active while we are awake, we would be materialists, for we would then equate the physiological activity of the brain with thinking. But if we are sensible people, we cannot say that the brain is more active in the waking state than in sleep. It must come to rest when we are awake.

Therefore the physiological activity in us cannot lead to thinking. If it could, thinking would have to result in a stronger physical activity than the non-thinking phase.

However, it is the absence of thought activity that is accompanied by an increased physical activity. Therefore we can say that our lungs would be lazy and inactive if oxygen from the outside did not reach them and activate them. Similarly, the brain is lazy during the day, and consequently something must reach it from the outside and activate it. Just as oxygen activates the lungs, so something coming from outside the body, something that is not in our body, must reach the brain during the day and initiate thinking there.

We see here that proper scientific thinking leads us of necessity to assume the existence of non-physical forces, of soul forces. After all, we have just seen that they exist. When we wake up, we see them move into us, as it were, for thinking cannot come from our bodies. If it could, we would necessarily be able to think much better at night. Thinking would then begin after we lie down and fall asleep. But that is not what happens. Rather, at the time of waking up, we sense something move into us: our soul and spirit being.

Granted, science has made considerable progress recently. However, it has learned only about things that are unsuitable for life itself and for thinking. Science has not understood life itself, and thinking even less. If we pursue natural science in the right way, it will be this true science, not some sort of superstition, that leads us to the realization that just as there must be oxygen for the breathing so there must be something spiritual for thinking.

We will go into this again next time because it is not a simple matter. Many of you will object strongly to what I have just said. But those who say something different do not comprehend what is really going on in the human being. It is therefore not a question of spreading some kind of superstition, but of establishing a clear understanding. That is what really matters.

The human being in relation to world-formation and dissolution

A member of the audience brought some rocks back from his holiday. He asked whether they, too, contain life or ever had life and how they originated.

Rudolf Steiner: Maybe I can refer to these rocks later, but I may also be able to include them in today's discussion.

What I wanted to say today, gentlemen, is the following: we have seen that life must constantly come to an end inside us. We also discovered that we have these organisms floating in our blood, the white corpuscles, which move through the arteries right up to our skin. I have told you also that these small creatures, which normally live everywhere inside our organism, are particularly pleased when they reach the surface of the body. It is like the spice of life for them. Those are the living cells moving around inside us.

In contrast to them, the cells in our nervous system, especially the brain cells, are constantly dying, constantly on the verge of death. The only time when they are alive to some extent is actually when we are asleep. They cannot move from their places because they are all crowded together. They cannot move around like the white blood cells, but at night, when we are asleep, they begin to be alive. Then they receive a bit more life and will forces from the body, and that is why the white corpuscles have to be more still and less active at that time. As I explained, this is how thinking occurs in the entire body.

Let us ask now where thoughts actually come from. As you know, people who want to think only in materialistic terms, that is to say, conveniently and superficially, say that thoughts clearly originate in the brain or in the nervous system. There thoughts grow like heads of cabbage in a field. If people were only to think this through — this picture of cabbages in a field — they would realize that no cabbages will grow in a field unless someone has planted them first. I don't object if people picture the human brain as a sort of field in which thoughts grow. But just think what would happen if the farmer who has always cultivated this wonderful patch of cabbage moved away, and there was no one to continue his work. Well, no more cabbages would grow on this field.

It is precisely when we assume that our thoughts originate in the brain that we must first find out where they really come from. Well, they come about the same way that heads of cabbage grow in a field! In other words, we must first get a proper grasp of the question, and then we will realize that what we see out in nature has indeed evolved there. I'd like to explain to you at this point what it is that evolves in nature.

As I mentioned earlier, we can understand the inner nature of human beings by looking at the world around us. As we studied the plants, we also gained some insights into human beings. Now let us look closely at this rock here. On the outside, on top, back, and bottom, it consists of very soft material. You can scrape it off with a knife. Thus the outer layer is almost like compacted soil. I'll draw only the lower part of it for you. Down here we have this soft stone material, and there are various crystals growing out of it, as it were. I would really have to draw many of them of course, but this will do for now.

Down there we have numerous small crystals that appear to have grown out of the other, softer material, but they are very hard. You cannot scrape them off; a knife will not scratch them. You may be able to remove one as a unit, but you cannot scratch into them. The crystals embedded here are very hard.

How did such crystals get into the softer material, which is really only compacted soil? The crystals are beautifully formed; they have an elongated shape and are crowned with a small roof. The opposite end would also have such a roof if it did not extend into the soil. Each crystal would have such a shape; but it is destroyed by entering more compact soil.

Where do these crystals come from? You know, don't you, that for plants to grow there must be carbon dioxide in their environment? They cannot grow without it. The plants must have the same substance we exhale. They absorb it, retain the carbon, and release the oxygen. This is the difference between us and the plants: we inhale oxygen and exhale carbon dioxide, retaining the oxygen. Plants are connected with the soil, and when they die the carbon returns into the soil, where over time it becomes hard coal, which we can mine many centuries later.

Of course, there are many other substances; for instance, one that resembles coal in some respects but is quite different from it in others is silica. If you have soil that is rich in silica and you have oxygen, which is always everywhere, the latter does not immediately affect the silica. However, after some time has passed in the natural course of things, we realize that the oxygen has united with the silica. Just as carbon dioxide develops when we breathe out, so quartz or silicate develops when oxygen unites in the right way with the silica in the soil. That is how those crystals originate; all that is needed is that the silica in the soil unites with the oxygen.

However the oxygen cannot unite with the silica by itself. No matter how much silica and oxygen you have, the two by themselves would not form anything at all. How then do these beautiful shapes develop? They develop because the earth is connected with the universe, and forces from there constantly affect it. These forces work upon the earth all the time. They carry the oxygen into the silica, and that is how crystals come about. Thus, crystals develop due to the influences of all the other stars upon the earth. We can therefore say that crystals are being formed here by forces from the entire universe.

Now you may wonder if I've been telling you tales. You may think the rock one of you brought proves the opposite of what I've said. However, this is what rocks are really like; let me draw it now for you [see drawing below]. In the lower portion there is loose soil, and also above and back there. The rock is entirely surrounded by loose earth. The crystals not only grow upward, as I have described them, but there are also some growing in the opposite direction.

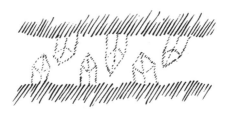

Now you may object that this process cannot be explained as the result of cosmic forces affecting the earth. For then one would necessarily have to assume that the same forces supposedly coming in from the universe must also emanate from the interior of the earth. Yes, you see, this is an apparent contradiction. There must be more to this than meets the eye. Let me tell you what it is.

Rocks like the one we have here do not develop just

anywhere in the soil, but only in the mountains. Even if they developed somewhere else and not in the mountains, there would be layers of earth above and below them, just like in the mountains. Let's assume we found this rock here in the mountains. Imagine now a mountain and a slope below it [*see drawing below*]. Now you are walking up there, and this is where the path must run, though the soil or the rocks may overhang the path a little bit.

A long time ago this soil was deposited up on the mountain in the drawing, and other soil was deposited down there on the path. If my explanation is true, then forces streaming in from the universe formed crystals up there as well as below. Both up there and down below crystals would have grown out of the soil. A long time later, the upper part of the rock [*upper left part of drawing*] broke off and covered the lower one. In the process, the soil came to lie on top of the crystals, which used to point upwards but now were pointing downwards and were pressing against the crystals below them, which were still pointing upwards.

Things like that happened in the mountains all the time. When you study geology, you will find that there have always been landslides in the mountains, and in the process the upper layers came to lie on top of the lower ones. This is what makes studying mountains so interesting. In the plains, where changes occurred only within the last millennia, you get the impression that one layer was always deposited upon the other. We cannot say the same about the Alps at all. A long time ago they began to develop in the same way, but later the higher portions fell on top of the lower ones, and the layers were all jumbled.

This is why it is difficult to study the Alps; one always has to ask whether the layers on top actually originated there. In many cases they did not. Instead, a lower stratum, covered by other layers, was often pushed to the surface by a seismic shock. What had been underneath thus came to lie on top of what used to be the topmost layer. The layers were inverted. This is how folded mountains, such as the Alps, developed over thousands of years.

To come back to our drawing, we can therefore say that something developed below the slope and something similar above it, which then slid down and covered the lower stratum. Thus we can explain the matter of crystals growing in opposite directions by pointing to the folded mountains and their origin in an inversion and jumbling up of strata.

The entire realm of inanimate matter is thus affected by forces working into it out of the universe. These forces work on us as well, and so we must actually do something to avoid their interference. For we also carry within us the silica we so frequently find in the earth. We don't have much of it, but nevertheless we do carry within us the same substances out of which very hard rocks can develop. But if hard rocks, such as the one we looked at a while ago, developed in our bodies, we would be in trouble! For instance, if as children, when we already have silica in us, we could not help but form these very small crystals, it would be a very serious matter. This is what sometimes happens in certain illnesses.

As you know, sugar can also form crystals. Rock candy, for instance, consists of layers of crystals, one on top of the other. Well, we have a lot of sugar in us. Yet, not all people on earth eat the same amount of sugar. The consumption varies. For example, on average people in Russia eat very little sugar, but in England they consume a lot. This creates one type of difference between people. The Russian folk character is different from the English one. The Russians are different people from the English, in part because they consume less sugar in their food. This connection between food and character has to do with the various forces that work upon us out of the universe.

So, human beings have a lot of sugar in them, and it constantly tends to turn into crystals. What can we do to prevent this crystallization?

As I told you, there is also a lot of water in us, living water. It dissolves the sugar. It would be quite something if the water did not constantly dissolve the sugar! Small crystals, as in rock candy, would develop, and if the sugar were not constantly dissolved, we would have such small pointed crystals everywhere in us. We need sugar in our food, but we can use it only by dissolving it continuously. We must have it. Why? In order to do the work of dissolving it! This is not the only thing that keeps us alive, but it is an essential part of human life to dissolve sugar. Therefore we must consume it.

If we have insufficient strength to dissolve it, very small crystals will form, which we excrete with the urine. This is a symptom of an illness called diabetes. Here we now have an explanation for why people succumb to this illness. They do not have enough strength to dissolve the sugar they have eaten. They must eat sugar, but when they are not strong enough to dissolve it, they will suffer from diabetes. The sugar must not get to the point where it is excreted in the form of minute crystals, but it must be dissolved. Human beings must have the strength to do this, for their life is based on this.

When we think about this, we realize that not only do we need to have the forces for dissolving sugar, but we also need to have the strength to break down the very tiny quartz crystals constantly tending to develop in us. They must not be allowed to form. If they were to develop in children, they would come and complain to us that they felt a stinging pain everywhere.

What has happened when a child feels this stinging pain all over? You see, in that case the tiny silica crystals that developed in the nerves were not dissolved. They remained intact. You must not imagine that they are large; they are extremely small, so that one can barely see them even under a microscope, smaller than the ten thousandth part of a millimetre. However, when many of these minute crystals have accumulated in the nervous system, the patient begins to suffer from countless minor stinging pains he cannot understand. He feels them everywhere. This process in turn leads to slight inflammations. The patient then becomes rheumatic, or he may also develop gout, which simply means that these tiny crystals are constantly being deposited. This is very painful. Tophi, or gouty concretions or nodes, are caused by inflammations such as you get when you stub your toe. The numerous tiny spears press towards the surface of the body. This produces minor inflammations which in turn lead to gouty nodes.

These are some of the processes that can occur in the human body. You see that we must always have forces in us that work against things like gout. If we did not have such forces, we would always succumb to gout. But we must not have gout all the time. Therefore we must always have something with which we can oppose it. You see, certain forces out of the universe work upon us. They want to form minute crystals within us. Since they permeate us constantly, we on our part must just as consistently develop the strength to counter these effects. We must oppose these forces all the time. This is particularly true in our nervous system, where mineral substances would develop continuously if we did not oppose them.

True, these mineral substances must develop; they are necessary. Autopsies of infants who were retarded and died young often reveal that the children did not have enough of what is called brain-sand. We all must have some of it. Brain-sand must develop, but it must also be dissolved again all the time.

If we don't have enough strength to dissolve this substance, too much of it will be deposited. In fact brain-sand is continuously being deposited in the brain as we absorb food through our blood. And this brain-sand is just as much subject to the influences of the forces of the universe as everything else out there in nature. Consequently the brain-sand too has the tendency to form crystals. But this must not be allowed to happen. Without brain-sand we may become retarded, but if crystals were to form we would always be fainting because we would suffer from some sort of rheumatism or gout of the brain. This crystal formation merely causes pain in the other parts of the body, but if the crystals develop in the brain, we grow helpless and faint. In other words, we must have brain-sand, but we must also dissolve it all the time. Forming brain-sand and dissolving it again is an ongoing process.

An excessive amount of deposits may occasionally rupture blood vessels in the brain, causing blood to flow out. This will not only cause fainting, but also a cerebral stroke or apoplexy. By studying illnesses, we can see what lives inside the human being. For when we are ill we have everything healthy people have in them, but we have it in excess. Simply put, illness is nothing else than developing something excessively.

This is true in life in general, gentlemen. If you gently touch a small child's cheek, you are caressing it. If the strength of your gesture becomes excessive, you are slapping the child. You see, this is the way things are in life. Whatever may be a caress can develop into a slap. Similarly, if the very delicate activity of depositing brain-sand becomes excessive, if we do not have enough strength to dissolve this mineral substance in us, it will turn into a slap given by life, so to speak. For we would constantly faint; or in the advanced stage, if these tiny crystals pierced our blood vessels, we would suffer apoplexy. This is the reason why we must dissolve them all the time; this process is constantly going on in all of us.

Let me tell you something else. To make things easier to understand, let's picture a human being; I'll make a drawing here. Here is the brain and the eye. Here I'll draw something that person is looking at, let's say a plant.

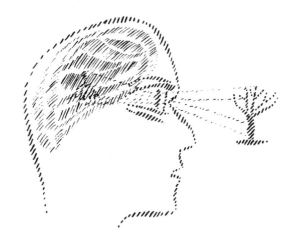

Now look at this plant. When we look at the plant—of course, we can do this only in the daytime, when there's light—we see that this plant is lit up by sunlight, and this light reaches all the way into our eyes. Through the optic nerve, which extends back from the eyes to the brain, the light reaches the brain. Thus, when we look at a plant, our eyes focus on it, and rays of light proceed from the plant through the eyes and into the brain.

Gentlemen, when you observe a plant, for example a flower, in this way, you are paying attention to it. To say that you pay attention to a flower is actually saying quite a lot. For when you focus on the flower, you forget your-selves. We can be so attentive that we completely forget ourselves. As soon as you begin to forget the fact that you are looking at the flower, the strength develops to deposit some brainsand in the brain. In other words, looking at something means depositing brain-sand.

This depositing is a typical process and part of being human. As you know, you perspire not only when you exert yourselves, but also, for example, when you are very frightened. Then you secrete not only brain-sand, but you also excrete other minerals and water through your skin. That is what is known as excretion. Looking at something means constantly excreting brain-sand. And as you know, we must dissolve this brain-sand, because if we did not this mineral would develop into a tiny flower in our brain! Looking at the flower actually means that the brain-sand in us forms a tiny flower; but it is an upside-down flower, just as the eye's picture of objects is upside-down.

When we look at a chair—it doesn't have to be anything as nice as a flower—through the act of concentrated looking a certain amount of brain-sand is formed in our head. If we now completely gave ourselves up to this act of looking, a very small picture of the chair, smaller even than anything you can see under the microscope, would develop in the brain-sand. If we had strengthened our faculty of con-centrated looking, and looked around in a room, the entire room would appear in our heads as an inverted image consisting of miniature silica grains. It is amazing what is constantly being built inside us. However, we don't allow it to be completed. Without being conscious of it, we keep destroying the structure.

In this respect, we are peculiar creatures. When we look at the things around us, they constantly want to form replicas of themselves in us, but upside-down replicas. Even if we did not take an interest in the world and did not look at things, such forms would be created in us by what happens in the universe, even at night when we are asleep and don't have the inner strength to dissolve those forms. These forms develop also when the earth is not illuminated by sunlight, but is affected by forces that come from much farther away. We are always vulnerable, susceptible to these forces.

When we are asleep, the cosmos wants to create all kinds of forms of the mineral, inanimate realm in us. And when we look at things, then shapes want to develop in us that are just like our surroundings. Thus, when we sleep we copy the cosmos, where everything is arranged the same way it is in crystals. Crystals look the way they do because cosmic forces are arranged in just the same way as the crystals. Some of these forces move in one direction, and others in a different one, so that crystals are shaped by the entire universe. This process wants to take place in us, too. When we look at the world around us, the shapes of our immediate environment tend to form themselves inside us as well. We must constantly prevent them from solidifying; we must constantly dissolve them.

Well, gentlemen, this is quite a strange process going on there. Just think, the flower wants to create an inanimate silica image of itself in us. But we must not let this happen. For if it did, we would not know anything about the flower, but suffer from gout in the head. Therefore the image must be destroyed before it solidifies.

Let me put it differently. Let's assume there is a pot of

lukewarm water in front of you. Then someone blindfolds you and brings an object that will dissolve in the water. You are now asked to put your hand into the pot. You cannot see the object, because you are blindfolded. You are then asked if you feel anything, and you answer that all you can feel is the lukewarm water. To the question if you feel anything else, you answer that you feel the water getting colder around your fingers now.

How did that happen? The other person put in an object that dissolved, and in the process the temperature of the water was reduced. You can feel the dissolving process around your fingers and can say that something is being dissolved in this liquid.

This is what happens constantly when we have formed the object in us and have to dissolve it again. We feel it dissolving, and we know that the object exists in our environment because it formed a picture inside us, which we in turn dissolved. And because we dissolved the image we also know what the object looks like. We can think about the object because we have first dissolved its image. That is how thoughts about the object can arise. If we had only the image we would faint. However, if we are strong enough to destroy the image, then we can know about the object. This then is the difference between fainting when we see something and knowing about what we see.

Let's consider the case of someone who is in poor health. When there is a sudden, tremendous thunder-clap — that can happen — then this thunder perceived with the ears, not the eyes now but the ears, leads to brain-sand being deposited inside the person, and a picture then arises. Now if this person can't destroy the image fast enough, he may faint, lose consciousness. If he were healthy this would not happen, because then he could dissolve the brain-sand quickly enough. In other words fainting means not diluting the brain-sand fast enough. Not fainting means dissolving it quickly enough. While perceiving our environment, we must keep dissolving the brain-sand quickly.

This leads us to the question of our relationship to cosmic forces. I told you last time that if our relationship to these forces is such that our brain cells are constantly on the verge of death, then these cells are obviously inanimate, and we must use them properly. It is with our soul-spiritual element that we use and control them. Now we find the force that constantly destroys our brain cells. It's the brain-sand that destroys them continuously. The brain-sand's interference in the brain cells kills them. We must oppose this process.

You see, this is the reason why we are human beings: so that in a certain way we can counteract the effects of the brain-sand. The situation is different in animals; they cannot counteract the brain-sand as human beings can. This is why the animals do not have a head like ours. The only exceptions in this respect are the highly developed species. The human head can constantly dissolve everything that enters it. This ability to dissolve everything that comes in enables us to perceive ourselves and thus to say 'I'. The dissolving of brain-sand is optimal when we can say 'I'. At that moment we permeate our language with consciousness.

All right then, the brain-sand and all the nerve-sand dissolve. This is not so in animals. That is why animals only manage to utter screams and similar sounds, but never speech. This is also why animals have no sense of self and cannot say 'I'. But human beings can, because they can dissolve the brain-sand to a much greater extent.

Thus we can say that we counteract not only what is on the earth, but also what reaches us from the cosmos. If we didn't do that, these forces from the universe would inwardly crystallize us. We would inwardly turn into a mountain system of superimposed layers of crystals. We oppose this process inwardly by constantly destroying these mineral forms. We not only dissolve the silicic acid in the form of these crystals, but we also dissolve all sorts of other things. For example, we dissolve the constituents of sugar among other things.

We can even trace these processes. Though we are not fully aware of these things because they proceed on a merely instinctual level, we vaguely sense them. Suppose now you feel that you have difficulties in thinking clearly, in keeping your thoughts together, in concentrating. This kind of feeling can easily overcome journalists who have to write an article every day. Well, gentlemen, writing an article per day means diluting a tremendous amount of brain-sand. What happens in such a situation — at least that's how it was in the old days — is that the person burdened with this terrible task of writing an article every day starts chewing the end of his pen. This is something journalists are said to do more than other people in order to gather energy. They rally their reserves from the entire body and direct them into their heads to overcome the brain-sand there. And a lot of brain-sand has to be dissolved.

All this takes place instinctively. Of course, journalists don't say that they chew on their pens in order to gather up thoughts. They do it out of instinct. Now, out of the same instincts journalists may go to a coffee shop and drink black coffee. They don't think much about it because they are not aware of these inner processes. But once they have had their coffee — my word, things really move! They can now write their stories.

Why is this so? Because they absorbed caffeine, a toxic substance that contains a lot of nitrogen. Nitrogen is also in the air. When we breathe, we always absorb a certain amount of oxygen and nitrogen. To dissolve brain-sand, we need a certain force that is to be found particularly in nitrogen. Out of the nitrogen we gather the forces to dissolve brain-sand.

That is the reason why we are more susceptible to nitrogen at night when we sleep than when we are awake. As we have said earlier, we live faster when we take in more oxygen. If we inhaled more nitrogen, we would live more slowly and be more awake. We would be able to dissolve more brain-sand.

The journalist who drinks coffee unconsciously counts on this nitrogen, which will enable him to form more brain-sand and to dissolve it more easily as well. This way his thoughts will line up properly, and instead of chewing on his pen he can now use it to write them down.

There you can see how the human ego works. When the stomach receives the caffeine, which is rich in nitrogen, the ego then moves the nitrogen into the brain. Thus it makes diluting the brain-sand easier and helps us to think coherently.

On the other hand, some people's thoughts tend to be too closely connected. These people are unable to free themselves from their own thoughts. They have a tendency to constantly work on their brain-sand and would be better off if they underwent the opposite process. While some people keep their thoughts coherently connected by following a train of thought, others require the help of caffeine for that purpose. However, people who don't want to keep their thoughts too tightly connected and controlled, but want to have them shine, to put on a brilliant show and, as we say, dazzle others with their thoughts, those people will drink tea. Here we find the opposite effect. Tea scatters their thoughts and supports the dissolving of brainsand in a different way.

The processes taking place inside us are extremely interesting and complex. Every type of food has a different effect, and we must constantly create a counterbalance to what tends to develop. We must in turn destroy what develops. It is actually with our highest spiritual capacity that we dissolve what tends to develop within us.

If for some time we do not get enough nitrogen in our diet, we will tend to be very sleepy. This is what one of you asked me about earlier, and the sleepiness is the result of not taking in enough nitrogen with our food. Therefore, when we are often sleepy we must take in food that is rich in nitrogen. There are many ways to do this, but we get nitrogen especially when we eat cheese or eggs. These will raise our nitrogen level. This is how we have to work to balance processes in us and to allow the ego to work in us.

As I told you at the beginning of today's talk, there may be fields with cabbages growing in them. But the cabbages won't grow if people don't cultivate them. And the field must also be prepared properly. Similarly, our brain must contain the required substances so that the ego can work there. The ego is also connected with all the forces of the universe, which work in a different direction. These cosmic forces want to make us into hard rocks, and we must counteract their effects in us all the time. If we could not do that, we would not be able to think or reach self-awareness. This activity of dissolving is identical with what we call our ego-consciousness.

You see, gentlemen, we must first answer these questions in a sensible way before we can go on to a scientific world view, before we can understand our relationship to the world. This dissolving is the most important aspect we must understand about ourselves. Let us think for a moment of a person who is dying. As a physical being he is entirely destroyed. If we do not understand that at every waking moment of our lives there is a process of destruction going on in us, we will never comprehend the destruction in a person who dies. We are able to continuously dissolve substances inside us because we oppose the cosmic forces in us. However, the dissolving is offset repeatedly because we take in the substances required for this activity with our food. If the point is reached where we can no longer dissolve the substances in us, we will dissolve ourselves and become corpses. We will talk more about that when we meet again.

What we found out today was that there is a constant dissolution process taking place and that we may become unable to dissolve the substances the universe tends to form in us because of an insufficient nitrogen balance. In that case the ego faints or becomes sleepy. Sleepiness means that we cannot dissolve sufficiently and are overcome by the forces of sedimentation.

When you fall asleep you are still there, because you can wake up again. By the same token, you must not draw conclusions concerning spiritual facts from what happens outwardly in your body. Just as a machine cannot do anything when nobody is there to operate it, so nothing happens in human beings without the presence of the spirit. This is a scientific view, gentlemen; anything else is unscientific. I am not telling you tall stories; on the contrary, everyone who takes this matter seriously and considers it scientifically will come to this insight.

We will continue these discussions in early September. You will see that this approach will, despite various detours, help us understand human beings in everyday life. Because of the basic understanding you have now developed, you will find it easier to follow. Remember, the human being is constantly being reconstituted, then dissolves himself, and so forth. When we study these things further in the future you will discover how a true scientist sees the human being.

The human being as body, soul, and spirit. Brain and thinking. The liver as organ of perception

Well gentlemen, as quite a bit of time has elapsed since my last lecture, I would like to review what we talked about last time. We discussed sleeping and waking and the connection between them. I also mentioned that we have very small organisms or cells in our brains, and I made a drawing of them for you. These cells consist of a body made of protein that extends into a star shape [*see below*]. These extensions are of varying lengths. Close to the first organism we find another one with its arms and so forth. These extensions or arms intertwine and form a mesh. This is why

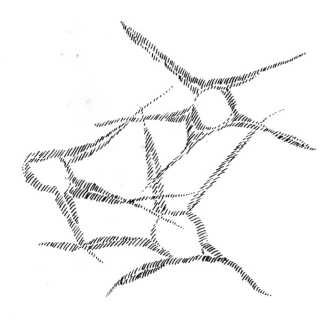

we find that the brain is actually a mesh containing these tiny dots when we look at it through a strong microscope. The most striking thing about these brain cells is that they are almost dead. Small creatures such as these brain cells would move if they were fully alive. I also spoke about another type of cell, the white blood corpuscles. They look like small creatures, and that is what they are. And like small creatures, they float around and feed. If there is anything in the blood that they can absorb, they extend their feelers and suck it in. They float and move through our bodies, and thus there are organisms floating around in our blood that are half dead and half alive.

When we are awake, the brain cells are really just about lifeless. And it is only because of this that we are able to think. If the brain cells were more alive, we would not be able to think. We can see that this is so when we consider that the brain cells are more alive when we are sleeping. It is precisely when we are not thinking but sleeping that they begin to live. They do not move around because they are too close to each other, too much crowded together. If this were not so and they had begun to move, we would not wake up at all.

When we examine the brain cells of a person who had lost his mental faculties and then died, we find that they had begun to live and to proliferate. They are softer than those in normal people. This is why in the case of mental deterioration we often speak of 'a softening of the brain' and that term is not such a bad one.

When we study living human beings objectively, without prejudice, we must admit that the life in our body cannot give rise to our thinking. On the contrary, this physiological life must actually die in the brain to enable us to think. That's the way it is. If our scientists were to proceed in the right way, they could not possibly be materialists. Based on the physical constitution of human beings they would

realize that mental and spiritual activities are most pro-
nounced precisely when the physiological processes fade
away, as they do in the brain. The existence of soul and
spirit can thus be proved in a strictly scientific way.

At night, when we sleep, our brain cells are more active,
and that is why we cannot think then. When we are awake
the white blood corpuscles begin to be active. This is the
difference between sleeping and waking. In other words,
when we are awake, when our brain cells are paralysed and
nearly dead, then we can think. When we sleep we cannot
think, because our brain cells begin to come to life, while
our white blood corpuscles approach a lifeless condition.
As far as our body is concerned, we actually need to have
something of death in us in order to be able to think and to
have a soul life.

You see, gentlemen, it is not surprising that modern science does not discover such things, because it developed in
a particular way. When you visit the university of Oxford,
as I was able to do recently when I gave a series of lectures
at that famous English university, you will be struck by the
fact that the university of Oxford is quite different from
those in Switzerland, Austria or Germany. Oxford University still has something medieval about it; it has a clearly
medieval character. For example, the graduating Ph.D.
candidates wear a gown and a mortarboard. Each university has its own style for these items. You can distinguish
an Oxford graduate from a Cambridge one, because their
gowns and mortarboards are different. Scholars there must
wear these things at certain formal occasions so that
everybody knows which university they attended. This is
because in England many medieval customs have been
preserved. For example, judges must wear a wig when
presiding in court. Many medieval customs have survived
in England and are still a part of people's lives. This is not
the case on the Continent, for instance in Switzerland,

Austria and Germany. Here students do not wear a gown when they graduate and judges no longer wear wigs.

Visitors from the Continent find these things funny and think that the British people are still living in the Middle Ages. These graduating scholars walk in the streets wearing their gowns and mortarboards. Yet there is more to it than meets the eye. You see science is still pursued there as it was in the Middle Ages. Compared to other, more modern universities that have abolished the old ways, the British universities are very nice — mind you, I don't want to argue for a return to gowns, but there is something very nice, something whole and complete about universities such as the one in Oxford.

They have preserved the Middle Ages in all their forms, and this gives a sense of completeness. For in the Middle Ages students at universities were allowed to explore anything they wanted except for the realm of religion. This is something you can sense even today in Oxford. If you were to talk about the supersensible world, people there would treat you with extreme reserve.

Well as long as they did not go into religious matters, medieval scientists had complete freedom, something we have lost. At our universities you have to be a materialist nowadays. If you are not, people treat you like a heretic; and if it were acceptable still, they would even burn you at the stake. You can see very clearly how people are treated who try to introduce something new into any of the scientific disciplines. To all appearances the wigs of formality have disappeared, but they continue to dominate people's attitudes here.

The sciences that developed on the Continent have kept many formal habits of the past and have become materialistic because they never dealt with spiritual matters. As I said, medieval scientists were not supposed to work with questions of the spirit, because this field was left to religion to explore. Nowadays people continue this division. They deal merely with the physical body and therefore do not learn anything about the spiritual nature of the human being. It is due only to the negligence of science that what is certainly there is not really studied.

I'd like to give you an example so that you see that anyone nowadays engaged in true science can indeed state scientifically that a soul or spirit enters the foetus in the mother's womb and leaves the human body again at the moment of death. We can now prove this scientifically, provided we really know our science and use it objectively.

But what does modern science do in specific instances? Let us say, for instance, that a person of 50 has a liver disease and dies because of it. Then an autopsy will be performed, the belly will be opened, and the liver will be examined. The pathologists may find that the inside of the organ has hardened a bit, and they will try to find out how this happened. At most, they will wonder what this person had been eating, based on the assumption that the liver may have hardened because of an inadequate diet. But nature is not that easy to understand. It is not enough to examine a person's liver and then to assume we found the reason for his illness. By merely investigating the last few years of a person's life, we cannot find out why the liver was in such a bad condition.

If you find that the liver of a 50-year-old person has hardened, the reason for that is usually—not always, but usually—that as a baby this person was fed the wrong kind of milk. Often what shows up as illness at the age of 50 was caused in very early childhood.

Why is this so? You see, if you really examine the liver and know its significance, you will realize first of all that in a very young child this organ is fully intact and actually still developing. Now the liver is quite different from all our other organs; it is unique. You can see this even from the outside. If you take any other organ, for example, the heart or the lung, you can see that it is an integrated part of the body. Let us think, for instance, of the right lung. You can see that arteries go in here and that veins come out there. The arteries bring in the oxygen, which is absorbed by the body, and the veins carry used blood; they contain carbon dioxide, which must be exhaled [*see drawing below*].

You see, every organ—stomach, heart, and so forth—is structured in such a way that it receives arterial blood and expels venous blood. This is not so in the liver. At first everything looks the same here as in the other organs. The liver, as you know, is located below the diaphragm on the right side of the body. Initially we find that here, too, arteries carry blood in and veins move blood out. If this were indeed all there is, the liver would be an organ like all the others.

But, unlike any other organ, we also find here a large blood vessel that carries venous blood, rich in carbon dioxide, *into* the liver. This so-called portal vein is quite big. It branches out into many smaller vessels inside the liver, supplying it with venous blood, which has become unsuit-

able for any other activities and which is normally cleansed
when we exhale carbon dioxide. Yes, we constantly send
carbon dioxide into the liver because it requires what all the
other organs must discard.

This is so because the liver is a kind of inner eye.
Especially when it is still fully intact, as in a child, the liver
senses not only the taste, but also the quality of the mother's
milk taken in. Later on in life, it will perceive every aspect of
the food we take in. The liver is an organ of perception; one
could also say it is an eye or a sentient organ. The liver
perceives many things.

Another organ of perception is the eye. It perceives the
world around us so strongly because it is almost isolated in
our head. It nestles into the orbital cavity and is thus almost
completely separate from the rest of the body. Our other
senses do not connect us as much with our environment as
the eyes do. If you hear something, you also have an inner
experience. This is why listening to music is more an inner
experience than seeing something. In contrast, our eyes are
arranged in such a way that they form less part of our body
and belong more to the world around us.

Normally venous blood gives off carbon dioxide to the air
around us and becomes oxygenated again. However, as I
mentioned earlier, the blood lacking oxygen flows into the
liver and thus makes this organ very different from the rest
of the body, just as the eyes are. The liver, then, is another
sense organ. The eyes perceive colours; the liver perceives

whether the sauerkraut I eat and the milk I drink are good or bad for my body. The liver perceives these things in a very discriminating way and then secretes bile, just as our eyes secrete tears. When we are sad, we start to cry. It is not without reason that the tears come out of our eyes. Becoming sad is connected with perceiving. Similarly, the secretion of bile is connected with the perception of the liver as to whether something is good or bad for the body. The extent of bile secretion depends on how harmful something is which we have taken in.

Imagine now that a child is given unwholesome milk. This will constantly irritate the liver. The infant may still be so healthy and strong that he does not immediately succumb to jaundice due to excessive bile secretion. However there will be a constant tendency in the child to secrete bile. Thus the liver becomes ill already in early childhood. Well, human beings can cope with a lot. This sick liver may last for another 40 or 45 years. But finally, in the fiftieth year, things come to a head: the liver has hardened.

Therefore it is simply not good enough to put the corpse of a 50-year-old man onto the autopsy table, open the belly, examine the organs, and then make a statement about them. In such a situation you simply cannot say anything worthwhile. Human beings are not just how they appear at any one moment; they develop over a number of decades, and that must be taken into account. And something that began long ago may express itself only 50 years later. In order to understand this, you have to know all about the person involved.

Let's assume now that you are materialists. Remember, I told you that the liver is an organ whose illnesses may have been caused at the infant stage, though they may not become noticeable or acute until the age of 50. What is going on there? Well, for simplicity's sake let's assume human beings only consist of flesh, blood, muscles, and so on.

Human beings have blood vessels, arteries, nerves, and so on. All of these consist of tissue or cells, of course. But do you actually believe that the tissue in an infant's liver will still be there at the age of 50? No, it will not.

Let me explain this with a simple example: you trim your fingernails, because if you didn't they would grow as long as a hawk's talons. So you regularly cut off pieces of your own body, you can say. When you get your hair cut, you again have part of your body removed. But that is not all. You will also have noticed that tiny pieces of skin, called dandruff, come off when you have not washed your hair for a while and scratch your scalp. If you were not to wash thoroughly for some time, and if your perspiration did not wash away very small pieces of skin, your entire body would be covered with scales. Yes, we constantly lose pieces of our body at its surface.

What happens when you trim off a piece of your finger-nail? The nail will grow back to that point again. It grows from the inside. This is typical of the entire human body. Tissue that was at one time innermost will reach the surface of the body after about seven years. Then it is discarded in the form of tiny flakes of skin or dandruff. Nature does this to us all the time, but we normally do not notice how these particles are discarded. The tissue in our body constantly moves from the inside to the periphery and there is sloughed off. What is deep inside your body today will have reached the surface in seven years and then will be discarded, and new tissue will have been formed inside you. Every seven years the soft tissues of the human body are renewed.

In the case of infants, this holds true even for certain bone structures. This is why we have our milk teeth only until the age of seven. Then they come out, and new teeth grow. We keep these second teeth only because we no longer have the strength to discard them, as we do our fingernails. Mind you, I know it is true that nowadays we do not tend to keep our second teeth all that long either. Especially in Switzerland, people suffer from tooth decay. This deterioration has to do with the water, particularly in our area.

This shows you that the tissue presently in your body will not be there seven years from now. You will have discarded it and replaced it with new material by that time. If it were merely a question of tissue, Mr Dollinger, who is sitting here with us, would not be the same person today he was seven years ago; for the material that made up his body then has completely disappeared by now. As far as tissue is concerned, he has become a different person. On the other hand, people addressed him by the same name seven years ago, and today he is still the same person, even though the cells within him have changed.

We can certainly see this tissue, for instance, when we dissect a corpse. But the forces that hold the tissue together, move it around, and replace it, these forces working all through us, we cannot see. They are what we call super-sensible forces.

Yes, gentlemen, when an infant's liver has been damaged and finally causes serious illness at age 50, this organ inside the body has been completely renewed in the meantime. The original material that made up the liver is no longer there. Thus, the cause for the liver disorder does not lie in the tissue itself, but in the invisible forces. When the person in question was still an infant, these forces usually prevented the liver from functioning normally. Not the tissue, but the functioning, the activity of the organ, became unbalanced. If we understand this in the case of the liver, we have to conclude that, since we constantly renew tissue, we also carry something in us that is not tissue, not matter.

If we fully grasp this idea, we will find it impossible to be materialists, for scientific reasons. Only people who believe that human beings are made up of the same material at age

50 as they were in infancy can be materialists. As you can see from the example I gave you, purely scientific reasons compel us to assume a spiritual basis to human life, a spiritual quality in human beings.

In other words, gentlemen, you cannot seriously believe that the original particles, long gone after 50 years, had anything to do with building and forming the liver. After all, they have been expelled from the liver. The only thing that remains of these particles now is the space they used to take up. What continuously rebuilds the liver is a force, is something supersensible.

In the same way, the entire body must be formed and constantly re-formed even before human beings can be born. The forces that work upon the liver must already be active when the foetus develops in the mother's womb. Of course, you can say that in the fallopian tubes the egg cell unites with the sperm cell, and then the human being begins to develop. Well, gentlemen, a human being can develop just as little out of this union of cells as, at age 50, a liver disease can develop out of tissue that was damaged in the first year of life. Granted, the material must be there. However, people who claim that human beings develop in the womb out of cells might just as well say that if I put down a few pieces of wood here and sit next to them for a few years they will then turn into a beautiful statue. Naturally, spiritual forces must have the material to work with; this is provided in the mother's womb. But human beings are not really formed there. It would be more accurate to say that like the wood carved by a sculptor, this material is shaped by spirit forces, thus giving rise to what continuously renews us when tissue is sloughed off or excreted. If matter were more important, we would not have to eat as much as we do. Although as children we would have to eat to grow, after having grown to adulthood at about age 20, we wouldn't have to eat anything any more if the tissue in us remained unchanged. This would be a wonderful thing for employers, because children are not allowed to work yet and adult workers would not need anything to eat! But we have to eat even when we are fully grown. This proves that what remains unchanged in human beings during their entire lifetime is not the original cell material, but the soul-spiritual forces. They must be present before conception can take place and must work on matter in us from the beginning to the end of our existence.

After birth, in early infancy, humans sleep almost continuously. In fact healthy infants should not be awake for more than one or two hours. Normally babies want to sleep most of the time. What does it mean that infants have a constant need to sleep and should do so? This means that their brain should still have a bit of life in it, and the white blood cells should not rush through the body too actively. They should still be at rest and the brain cells should be relatively active. This is why infants must sleep. Of course, they cannot think yet. As soon as they begin to think, the brain cells begin to become increasingly lifeless. As long as we are growing, the same forces that support our growth also maintain our brain in a soft, physiologically active condition. But once we stop growing or slow down, these activating forces find it ever more difficult to reach the brain even during sleep. The result is that as we get older, we learn to think better, but our brain tends more and more to approach a condition close to death. Once we have grown up, there are actually death processes going on in the brain all the time.

Of course, we are hardy creatures. For a long time after growing up, we are able to make our brains sufficiently soft at night. But there comes a time when the forces streaming up into the head can no longer supply the brain properly; then it will begin to age.

What do people actually die of? It is true, of course, that

once an organ is damaged or destroyed the spirit forces can no longer work through it, just as we can no longer work with a machine once it is out of order. But apart from that, the brain becomes more and more hardened with age and more and more difficult to reconstitute to its earlier softness. During the day, the brain is constantly being worn out, because it is not the body that rejuvenates the brain, but the soul-spirit forces. But these influences are, as it were, like poison. In the waking state, the brain is being undermined by the soul-spirit forces. We must sleep in order to allow the brain to be reconstituted, rejuvenated. If the brain were unable to think, it would not be worn out but become ever stronger. For instance, the arms do not think, but work and therefore grow ever stronger. In contrast, the brain becomes weaker and weaker due to the thinking going on there. The brain does not think because of its physiological vitality but because of the death processes in it, and therefore our whole body eventually becomes unusable. The spirit is present, but the body is eventually no longer usable.

The same development can be seen in what I talked about earlier, in the liver. It functions in our body like an eye, like a sense organ. Yes, gentlemen, if the liver of a 50-year-old person has become as hardened as I described, it is ill. But there is always a slight hardening of the liver as we get older. Only in children is the liver still very soft. It consists of minute, interconnected reddish-brown lumps of tissue, the so-called liver tissue. This tissue is supple and soft in early childhood, but the older we get the harder it becomes. Just think of the eyes for a moment, where the same thing occurs. As we get older, the inside of the eye gradually hardens. In its pathological extreme, this leads to glaucoma. Similarly, excessive hardening of the liver leads to cirrhosis accompanied by abscesses and so forth.

But even if we remain healthy, the liver gets worn out through normal wear and tear in its function as a sense organ, just as the eyes do. Because of this deterioration, the liver becomes less and less capable of perceiving whether the food we eat is good for us or harmful. Once we have grown old, the liver helps us less and less to judge how useful the substances are that have entered the stomach. This function is no longer being fulfilled properly. When it is healthy, the liver is responsible for distributing beneficial substances throughout the body and keeping harmful ones away. When the liver begins to deteriorate, however, it can no longer prevent all harmful substances from entering the intestinal glands and the lymph. From there they are spread throughout the entire body and cause various illnesses.

This gradual drop in the vitality of the liver makes it more and more difficult for older people to perceive their body inwardly as they used to. One could say that in relation to their own body they have become blind. If you are blind to the outside, someone else can guide you and help you. But if you become blind inwardly, your physiological processes don't work properly, and soon that will lead to cancer of the intestine, the stomach, the pylorus, or to some other disorder. Then the body is no longer usable. In addition, the new tissue that has to be replaced constantly can no longer be properly integrated into the body. In other words, the soul is no longer able to work on the body as it used to, and the time comes when the body as a whole must be discarded.

Actually, the body is being given up from year to year. For example, when we slough off dandruff from our scalp or trim our nails, we discard material that has become unusable. But the forces working in us remain. However, once the body as a whole becomes unusable, these forces can no longer replace anything. Just as the nail material, dead skin cells, and so forth were discarded from the body before, so now the entire body is discarded. All that remains of the human being then is the spirit. Thus, if we understand human beings at all, we have to understand them as consisting of body and spirit. We have to recognize that it is wrong to see the human being as a merely physical being.

You may want to argue now that this is only a matter of religion. But it is not just a religious matter at all. The science we pursue here at the Goetheanum clearly shows that we are not just dealing with a question of religion. Religion is supposed to comfort us in our fears by assuring us that we do not die when our bodies die. Basically, these are selfish fears, and the priests count on them. Therefore they tell us that we will not die. Here, however, we are not dealing with a religious matter, but with something eminently practical. Let me explain this.

People dissecting a human liver don't think about how important it is to feed infants properly. But those who realize how these things work will find ways of bringing up children in such a way that they become healthy human beings. It is much more important to establish health in childhood than to heal illnesses later. But people do not know anything about this, because they see the human being as nothing but a pile of tissue. Well, I believe the last example illustrates fairly well what I have been trying to say.

Let us now use a different case. Let's assume a child of school age is made to learn so much that his memory is overburdened, so that the child can't come to his senses, as it were. Yes, gentlemen, this definitely puts a strain on the child's spirit. But there is more to it than that; after all, the spirit constantly works upon the child's body. If we continue to teach and educate this child in the wrong way, for instance, by overdoing memory work, we will cause certain organs of his to harden, simply because the forces channelled to his brain will be lost to the other organs. Putting too much strain on a child's brain may lead to kidney disease. In other words, illnesses may be caused in a child not only through physical imbalances but also through the way we teach and educate.

As I said, here the matter becomes eminently practical. If we really understand the human being, we can apply proper pedagogy in our schools. If, however, we view human beings as modern scientists do, the universities will only teach what I mentioned earlier, namely, that the liver looks like this and consists of minute reddish-brown lumps of tissue and so forth, but beyond that they have nothing to say.

This science is impractical because it cannot be carried into our schools. Teachers cannot make use of such a science. But they can apply a science that tells them what a healthy liver looks like at age 30, and that to allow this healthy development of the liver they have to do certain things with their eight- or nine-year-old. pupils. Then they'll know not to demand that children learn exclusively through instruction with visual aids, but to teach them in such a way that the children's organ development is stimulated and guided properly. For instance, they will tell stories and have the youngsters retell them in a way that will not overburden their memory forces but allow them to develop at their own pace. Teachers can do this, provided they understand the human being in body, soul and spirit. Out of such insight they can educate properly.

Let me ask you now whether there is not after all something far more important than preaching comforting sermons about a supernatural world to assuage people's fears of dying when their bodies do. We do indeed not die with our body, as I have demonstrated. However, priests generally only pander to people's egotistical desire to go on living. Science, on the other hand, has nothing to do with desires, but only with facts. Once we fully grasp them, these facts make this entire matter eminently practical. If we fully understand the human being, we can carry the right impulses into our schools and apply them there.

This attitude is what distinguishes the science pursued here at the Goetheanum from any other. Here we intend to gradually establish conditions that apply not only to a few scientists, but that will humanize the sciences in general so they can benefit all of humanity and help us develop in the right way.

Present-day science does not work on practical applications, except in technology and to some extent in certain other fields, such as medicine. For instance, universities teach theology or history. Well, gentlemen, let's ask whether these teachings are applied in life. A theologian cannot apply his science, not even in the pulpit, because he must preach what people want to hear. Or ask lawyers, attorneys and judges. They memorized all sorts of things for their exams. But later they will forget them as fast as they can, because the world out there is ruled by different laws. Of all this knowledge, nothing is applied to living human beings. In other words, the various disciplines of knowledge no longer have any practical relevance to life. And that is bad.

This, as you can see, leads to the formation of class distinctions between people. In life, everything living must be applied, must be used. Thus, if there is a science that can no longer be applied and is consequently useless, then the people involved in it, these scientists, are also in a sense useless; they form a redundant class in society. This is what I mean by class distinctions.

In *Towards Social Renewal: Rethinking the Basis of Society*, I tried to show that class distinctions are in fact also connected with our spiritual life.[1] But as soon as we point out the truth, everybody calls us dreamers. However, you can see for yourselves that we are not dealing with fantasies or dreams, but with true insights that allow the various sciences to be applied in life. These insights will perhaps also reassure people about death.

Some of this may be difficult for you to follow, precisely because our school education is not what it should be. But gradually you will understand what I have been saying. Rest assured that others, even today's top scientists, do not understand me any better. If I were to present the science pursued here at the Goetheanum at Oxford University today, it would be quite different from what is being taught there and would be understood only gradually and slowly.

I wanted you to see how difficult it is to spread these viewpoints. It is difficult indeed. But we will succeed as we must; otherwise humanity will simply perish.

The perception of thinking carried out by our inner organs

Gentlemen, what we discussed up to now is so essential to what I want to say today that I would like to begin with a brief review.

As you remember, we have seen that the human brain essentially consists of minute, starlike cells that radiate out quite far from the centre and intertwine, forming the brain tissue as I described it to you. We find similar small organisms also in our blood, but our brain cells are fully alive only at night when we sleep. However, they cannot make full use of this life and move around because they are crowded together like sardines. However, the white blood corpuscles swimming in our blood can move around. They float around in the blood and move their armlike extensions. They only come to rest and approach a deathlike condition when we sleep. In other words, sleeping and waking are connected with the activity or inactivity of the brain cells, the nerve cells in general, and the white blood cells.

I also explained to you that in an organ such as the liver we can see how the human body changes in the course of a lifetime. Last time I described the perceptive capacity of the liver through which it regulates our digestion. If an infant's liver function is disturbed, the liver cannot perceive the digestive process properly. As I indicated, the consequences of this imbalance often do not appear until much later, for instance, at age 45 or 50. After all, the human organism can withstand a lot of strain, and even if the liver is damaged in infancy, the organ can continue to function for another 45 or 50 years. But by then the liver has hardened, and liver diseases appear. Though these diseases often occur only late in a person's life, they are nevertheless the effects of what went wrong in infancy.

Thus the best food for infants is the milk of their mothers. After all, the baby developed in the mother's body, and therefore its entire organism is related to that of the mother. Consequently, infants thrive best if they are given only what proceeds from the mother's body, to which they are closely related.

Occasionally it happens that because of its particular composition the mother's milk is not suitable for the baby. For example, the milk may be too bitter or too salty. Then another woman must be found to nurse the child.

Now you may ask if the infant could not be raised on cow's milk from the very beginning. Although feeding cow's milk in early infancy is not ideal, it is nonetheless not a terrible offence against the human organism to use it in the proper dilution. Of course, the milk of each mammal species is different from that of the others, but not so different that we couldn't feed human infants with cow's milk.

As long as babies only drink milk, they do not need to chew anything. Therefore, at this age certain organs are more active than later when solid food has to be processed. The milk infants drink is essentially still alive, as it were. Infants should be fed liquid life, so to speak.

Now, you know that something extremely important for the human organism happens in the intestines. I am speaking of the fact that all substances entering the intestines through the stomach must first be destroyed and killed, and later, when they pass through the intestinal walls into lymph vessels and blood, they must be revitalized. This is the most important thing we must understand. The food we take in must first be killed and then filled with life again. The living substances we take in from the world around us cannot be used by our body. Through our own activity we must kill and then re-enliven all our food. Traditional science does not know this, and therefore it also doesn't know that human beings bear life forces within them. Just as we have muscles, bones and nerves in us, so we also have enlivening forces in us, that we may call life body or etheric body.

The liver watches over this entire digestive process, the destruction and re-enlivening of substances, and the absorption of the newly vitalized substances into the blood, just like our eyes watch the events around us. As we get old, our eyes may suffer from cataracts or glaucoma, that is, they may harden and what was once transparent may become opaque. Similarly the liver can harden with age. Hepatic induration is actually the same thing in the liver as glaucoma in the eyes. This hardening of the liver may occur at the age of 45, 50, or even later. Liver diseases generally indicate that the liver no longer watches over the processes inside us.

With our eyes we look at the world around us, with our ears we listen to the sounds of our environment, and with our liver we perceive our digestion and all related processes. The liver is our inner organ of perception. And only if we recognize the liver as an inner sense organ can we understand what happens inside us. We can indeed compare the liver with our eyes. We have, as it were, a head in our belly. This head, however, does not look outwards but inwards. Thus we are engaged in an inner activity of which we are not conscious.

But babies still sense this activity. They pay little attention to the world around them, and even when they do they don't understand it at all. That is why infants feel into themselves all the more. They can sense clearly when the milk contains foreign substances that must be expelled into the intestines so that they can be excreted. If something is wrong with the milk, the liver will develop the tendency to become diseased later in life.

Well, you don't need me to tell you that the eyes that look at the world around us also need a brain. Merely looking at things doesn't do us any good. Then we would only be staring at the world without being able to think about it. We need the brain to think about the world around us.

Now, gentlemen, if the liver is a kind of inner eye that perceives the processes in our intestines, it also needs a kind of brain. Granted, the liver can perceive what is going on in the stomach, for instance how all the food we swallowed is mixed with pepsin. When the resulting mush or chyme then moves through the pylorus and into the intestines, the liver can sense that the usable substances are absorbed by the intestinal walls and enter the blood via the lymph vessels. But beyond this point the liver cannot do anything. Just as the eye cannot think, the liver cannot carry out the activities following upon mere perception. In the same way that the brain must support the eye, another organ must step in here to help the liver.

Thus we have not only the liver in us, which constantly perceives our digestion, but there is also a thinking activity taking place in us of which we are not aware. Even though we know the organ involved, we are not conscious of this thinking activity that complements and supports the perceptive function of the liver, just as the thinking of the brain supports the perceiving activity of the eyes. This thinking supporting the liver is provided by the kidneys and the whole kidney system.

Usually all we know about the kidneys is that they excrete urine. But this organ is more important than we generally think. In addition to excreting liquids, the kidneys work together with the liver and carry out an inner thinking activity. This is connected with the thinking that takes place in the brain; a malfunction in the brain therefore also affects the kidneys.

Let's assume a child's brain doesn't function properly. As I said, this can happen if the child has to learn too much and has to memorize too much. A certain amount of memorization is good to keep the brain agile, but too much memorizing will put so much strain on the brain that it will begin to harden. This hardening in turn will later prevent the brain from functioning properly.

Now, since the brain is connected with the kidneys, the latter will also not work properly as a result of the brain malfunction. The human body can take a lot of abuse, but the effects will show up later. In this case, the entire metabolism is disturbed, the kidneys no longer function properly, and we can find that sugar, which should have been assimilated by the body, is excreted in the urine. The organism has become too weak to assimilate the sugar because the brain no longer works as it should. The person in question suffers from diabetes.

What I want to impress upon you here is that our health in later life depends on our mental activity, for instance on the amount of memorizing at an early age. You have surely heard that diabetes occurs frequently in well-to-do people, haven't you? Those people can provide very well for their children, particularly as far as material things and the physical realm are concerned. But usually they don't know that they also need to look for a good teacher who will not make their children memorize too much. They think the government will take care of this and don't bother themselves about it. However, their children often memorize far too much and will in later life suffer from diabetes. Education relying only on material means, on proper nutrition, and so forth is not enough to help children develop into healthy adults. We must also consider their soul qualities.

Gradually people are now beginning to sense that these

soul qualities are important and that there is more to human beings than just a body; after all, the body can be ruined by neglect of the soul. No matter how well children eat and how much their diet is based on the research of chemists, if their soul life becomes unbalanced and is neglected, their organism will be damaged. It is not through modern one-sided and materialistic science but only through true science that we will be able to understand what was present in the human being already before conception and what remains after death. Only through true science will we come to know the human soul. And it is precisely this that has to be taken into account here.

Why is it that nowadays people generally don't want to hear anything about what I have just explained to you? These days people with a certain kind of education consider it 'uncultured' to speak about the liver and the kidneys. Why is that so?

You know, the Jews in antiquity—they are the ones who gave us the Old Testament—did not think that talking of the kidneys was so terribly uncultured. Nowadays people are so well brought up that in respectable company they will not repeat what is written in the Old Testament, but we can read there that the Jews in antiquity when suffering from bad dreams did not say, 'My soul is tormented.' You see, gentlemen, it's easy to say that when one has no idea what the soul is. 'Soul' is then merely a word. But the Old Testament expresses a wisdom people used to have in ancient times when it says about a man's bad dreams, 'His kidneys torment him.' This knowledge that bad dreams indicate a malfunction of the kidneys—knowledge that was present in the Old Testament but then was forgotten—comes to light again in the new science, in anthroposophy.

In the Middle Ages, a new way of thinking developed that has prevailed into our times. In those days, people developed an appreciation for what they could not perceive, for the imponderable. As you know, we usually cover all of our body except the head, and in company we speak only of the parts that are not covered. Well, nowadays you can see many women, indeed, even well-bred ladies, leaving considerably more of their bodies uncovered; but of course, this doesn't mean that we may speak of everything that isn't covered. At any rate, for a certain sect of medieval Christians — in England they were later called Puritans — what is inside our body gradually became unmentionable, something one must not speak of. The science of the time, based only on material things and sensory perception, was not allowed to talk about the inside of the human body. It was considered not spiritual and therefore should not be talked about. This is how the spirit eventually was lost sight of altogether. For it is obviously difficult to get a hold on the spirit if one looks for it only in the head. But we can certainly find the spirit pervading the entire human body if we look for it there.

Now let's go back to the kidneys; through their thinking they support the perceiving activity of the liver. In other words, the liver perceives and the kidneys think. They can think their way into the heart activity as well as into anything else the liver has not perceived. The liver can perceive the entire process of digestion and the absorption of liquefied nutrients into the blood. But once they circulate there, thinking must be brought to bear, and this is what the kidneys do. Thus we can say that there is, so to speak, a second person inside us.

But, gentlemen, you won't actually believe that the kidneys taken from a corpse and then dissected — or the beef kidneys that you can even more easily examine before you cook them for your meal — that this piece of meat with all the qualities the anatomists attribute to it can really think, will you? Of course it can't think. The soul forces permeating the organ are what do the thinking.

That's connected to what I told you last time about matter and tissue. For example, the material that made up a child's kidneys will have been replaced after seven or eight years. Just as your fingernails are no longer the same after seven or eight years because you keep trimming them, so all the tissue in the kidneys and the liver has been replaced. In other words, the physical material that made up these organs seven years ago is gone.

Yet decades later the liver can still become ill as a result of neglect suffered in infancy. Clearly then, an activity is taking place here that is invisible and independent of the organ tissue, which has been replaced repeatedly. Life continues from infancy to the age of 45 or 50, but the physical material does not. The tissue itself cannot become ill because it is constantly being replaced. What continues is the invisible activity inside us that will continue throughout our whole life. As you can see, our body is indeed extremely complex.

Let me now add something else. As I said, the Jews in antiquity still knew that the kidneys participated in the vague and dull thinking that takes place at night in our dreams. Of course, at night there is none of our usual thinking going on, and we perceive only what the kidneys are thinking. During the day, we have our heads full with thoughts that come originally from the outside. As we don't see the small flame of a candle when a brighter light stands next to it, so we don't see the kidney activity's small light when we are awake and our heads are filled with all sorts of thoughts and ideas coming from the world around us. As soon as the head stops thinking, it begins to perceive what the liver observes and the kidneys think in the form of dreams. This is why our dreams are the way they are.

Let's assume you have an intestinal disorder, and the liver perceives it. During the day, you don't notice the problem because the impressions reaching you from the outside are stronger. But at night, before falling asleep or waking up, you notice the liver perceiving the intestinal disorder. The liver and the kidneys are of course not as intelligent as our head, and therefore they cannot immediately say, 'What we see here are the intestines.' Instead they create an image, and so we don't see reality, but have a dream. If the liver were to see reality, it would see the intestines burning. But it doesn't and instead forms a picture, for example of snakes darting their tongues in and out. We dream quite often of wriggling snakes because the liver actually sees our intestines as snakes.

Indeed, sometimes we also do with our head what the liver and kidneys are doing. For example, when we see a crooked piece of wood and know there could be snakes around, from a distance we may mistake the piece of wood for a snake. Similarly, the inner perception and thinking of liver and kidneys can mistake the coiled intestines for snakes.

Sometimes you may dream of a roaring stove, and when you wake up you feel your heart throbbing. What has happened there? Well the kidneys were thinking about the palpitation of your heart and thought of the heart as a warm, roaring stove. And therefore you were dreaming of a hot stove; that's how the kidneys thought of the activity of your heart.

Though it may not be considered 'cultured' to say this, nevertheless the fact is that there is a soul being in our bellies. The soul is like a tiny mouse that somehow slips into our body. That's how people used to think about where the soul can be found, isn't it? Of course, to ask where the soul can be found is to say that one no longer knows anything about the soul at all. It is just as much in our ear lobes as in our big toes, but the soul needs organs by means of which it can think and form images. The soul does one kind of thinking with the head, which you know very well, and another kind is done with liver and kidneys and focuses on the perception of what goes on inside us. We can see the soul at work everywhere in the human body, and that is what we must understand.

Naturally, to fully understand this we need a science that does not stop at merely dissecting corpses and analysing organs only in physical, material terms. We must be more active in our soul life and thinking than those people who merely want to look at things. Of course, it's much easier to dissect corpses, take out the liver, and then record what one finds in it. For this kind of thing you don't need to exert your brain very much. All you need to do is use your eyes and add a bit of thinking as you cut the liver into small pieces and look at them under a microscope. This kind of science is easy.

Unfortunately, nowadays almost all science is conducted at that simple level. We have to be much more active in our thinking and we must stop believing that we can come to understand the human being just by dissecting corpses and describing the organs we see. Merely looking at the liver of a 50-year-old man or woman does not tell us anything about developments that began already in infancy. What we need is a holistic, comprehensive science; that's what all true science should strive for. Anthroposophy strives to develop such a science that will not limit itself to the physical but will extend to the realm of soul and spirit.

As I said last time, unlike in all other organs, the blood vessels entering the liver carry venous blood, blood containing carbon dioxide. The liver is unique in this respect. It receives the venous blood and absorbs it. This is extremely important.

Of course, the liver also receives the usual arterial blood, and there are also veins coming out of the liver. But in addition to these, a particular vein, the portal vein, enters the liver, bringing it blood rich in carbon dioxide [*see drawing on page 55*]. The liver absorbs the carbon dioxide and retains it.

You see, when conventional scientists dissect the liver, they see this portal vein but do not really think much about it. But if they had advanced to true science, they would draw comparisons.

Certain other organs in our body are similar to the liver, namely, the eyes. Though we find only faint indications of this in the eyes, it is nevertheless true that here, too, not all the venous blood flows out again. Arteries enter the eyes, and veins come out. However, not all the venous blood that entered the eyes flows out again; instead it is spread throughout the eyes, just as it is in the liver, only to a much lesser extent. Doesn't this tell us that eyes can be compared to the liver? Yes, and we can indeed say that the liver is our inner eye.

Our eyes are directed outwards. They look at the world outside and use up the venous blood in this process. The liver uses it up in looking at what goes on inside us. It uses the venous blood for a different purpose and makes it disappear. You see, it is only sometimes that the eyes use the venous blood, that is when we become sad and cry. Then bitter tasting lacrimal fluid is secreted by the tear glands. When the small amount of venous blood retained by the eyes is activated through our sadness, we excrete tears.

In the liver this is happening all the time. The liver is in a constant state of sadness, and seeing the human body as it is during life on earth, one has good reason to be sad. For though endowed with the highest potential, our body simply does not look all that good from the inside. So the liver is simply sad all the time, and that's why it continuously secretes a bitter substance called bile. What the eyes do with tears, the liver does for the entire organism by secreting bile. The only difference is that the tears flow to the surface of the body and then soon evaporate. The bile does not evaporate in us since the liver looks at the inside of our body. Here the process of perception becomes less important than that of secretion, which can be compared with the excretion of tears.

Now, gentlemen, if what I said is really true, then certain other things must necessarily also be true. Above all, it would have to be true that animals, which live more inwardly, more in their inner thinking activity, are thinking not less than human beings but more. Of course, with their heads they would have to think less because their brains are less developed than ours. Consequently, these creatures would have to focus more on the activity of their liver and kidneys; their liver would have to perceive more and their kidneys would have to think more. In fact, this is what actually happens in animals, and there is external proof of it. Our eyes are structured so that only very little venous blood flows into them. The amount is so small that modern science does not even mention it any more. However, in animals, which live more inwardly, the eyes not only look at things but also participate in the thinking process.

We can say, then, that in a way the eyes are a kind of liver, and by the same token we can say that in animals the eyes are much more like the liver than in human beings. Our eyes are more developed and therefore function less like the liver. The eyes of animals do not just consist of the same elements as human eyes, that is, of the watery vitreous body, the lens, and another vitreous body. No, in the case of certain animals the blood vessels enter the eyes and there form a structure like the one I'm drawing here [*see opposite*]. The blood vessels extend into this vitreous body and there form a structure called 'fan' or 'eye fan'.* Thus in animals the eyes still function very much like the liver. Just as the

---

* At this point there is a gap in the transcript of this lecture.

portal vein enters the liver, this fan reaches into the eyes. This is what happens in animals: as soon as they look at something their eyes begin to think. In human beings on the other hand, the eyes merely perceive, and the thinking is done with the brain. The brain of animals is small and less developed, and that is why they cannot think as much with the brain and have to use their eyes to some extent for this purpose. They can do this because they have this sickle-shaped extension reaching into the organ, allowing them to use the venous blood, which is rich in carbon dioxide.

You won't be surprised when you hear what I have to say now; after all, you know better than to assume that a vulture circling way up in the sky can decide with its tiny bird brain to swoop down precisely to the spot where the lamb is sitting! If vultures had to depend on their brain they would starve to death. However, in their eyes a thinking takes place that is merely the continuation of the thinking going on in their kidneys. It is with this thinking that vultures decide to swoop down and strike the lamb. Vultures do not think this through step by step, from the perception of the lamb to getting ready for the attack to swooping down at just the right angle to catch the prey. No, this kind of deliberation requires a fairly developed brain. We could deliberate like that, but then we could not follow through on such thinking. In vultures the eyes are already doing some thinking; their soul is even in their eyes. Of course, the birds don't realize it but this thinking is nevertheless going on.

As I said earlier, the Jews in antiquity understood their Old Testament, and they knew what it meant to say, 'God has tormented me at night through my kidneys.' This is how they expressed the reality of what their souls perceived in dreams. They said, 'God has tormented me at night through my kidneys,' because they knew very well that human beings not only look at the world outside through their eyes, but they also look inwards with their liver and think there with their kidneys.

The people of ancient Rome still had this knowledge, too. They knew that every person is actually two human beings in one — one who looks out through the eyes and one who looks inside through the liver. If you look at the distribution of the veins in the liver, you'll see that, in a sense, the liver looks towards our back. This is why we perceive so little of what goes on inside us. Just as we can't see what is behind us, so the liver isn't fully conscious of what it is looking at. In ancient Rome people knew this, but they did not express it in a way one could immediately understand. Instead, they pictured human beings as having one head that looks to the front and another one, in the lower body, that is less clearly formed and looks to the back. Then they pictured the two side by side [*see drawing below*], as one head with two faces,

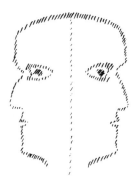

looking in opposite directions. You can still find statues of such Janus faces in Italy.

You see, tourists who can afford to travel through Italy with their guidebooks also look at those Janus faces. But when they consult their guidebooks about them, they don't find much useful information. After all, it is only natural to wonder how the Romans got the idea of sculpting such two-faced heads. They were certainly not so stupid as to believe that somewhere across the seas there lived people with two heads. Yet this is what tourists tend to think, because they don't learn anything different from just looking at those two-faced Roman heads.

Well, you see, out of a certain natural thinking the Romans still knew what later civilizations didn't know any more, and what we are now rediscovering on our own. Thus we know that the Romans were not stupid at all but quite clever. The Janus-face stands for January. Why did they place this figure at the beginning of the year? This question points to another mystery.

Now that we have come to the point of understanding that the soul works not only in the head, but also in the liver and the kidneys, we can also see how this activity varies in the course of the year. In the warmth of summer, for instance, the liver does little work. At that time, liver and kidneys enter a kind of soul sleep and carry out only their physical functions, because we surrender ourselves to the warmth of the world around us. In terms of soul activity, the entire digestive system is slower. But in winter soul-spiritual activities resume with renewed force. Around Christmas and New Year, at the beginning of January, the soul activity in liver and kidneys reaches its culmination. The Romans knew this, and that's why they called this two-faced being Janus, the January being.

When we rediscover the wisdom hidden in these statues, we won't just be staring at them, but instead we'll be able to understand them. Nowadays people can't do more than stare at those statues because modern science is no longer anything much. You see, anthroposophy isn't impractical in the least. It can shed light on the human being as well as on history. For instance, it can explain why the Romans made these Janus faces. And I can say without vanity that tourist guidebooks should actually be written by anthroposophists; otherwise tourists can only numbly stare at things without really thinking about them.

Well, gentlemen, from what I have said you can see that it is true that we must start with the body and its physiology to get to the soul and its realm. I will tell you more about the realm of the soul next Saturday, and in the meantime you can think of more questions to ask. For now I'm sure you realize that we are not joking when we try to understand and perceive the soul through the body; no, indeed, this is serious science.

The processes of digestion in physical as well as soul-spritual terms

To complete our picture of the human being, let's look more closely at what is going on every day in our body when certain processes take place. After all, we can understand more complex processes only after we have learned about the basic ones. This is why I want to discuss again the processes of nutrition in both their physiological and psychological aspects.

When we eat, we take in food through the mouth. We take in both liquid and solid substances, and by inhaling through the lungs we absorb gaseous ones. But our body can assimilate and use only liquids. Therefore all our solid food must be liquefied already in the mouth. This is accomplished by small glands in our mouth and palate that constantly produce saliva. You must picture them everywhere in the mouth cavity, even along the edge of the tongue. Seen under a microscope the salivary glands resemble small grape bunches because they consist of a cluster of many adjoining cells. They produce saliva, which in turn must dissolve and permeate all food in order to make it digestible.

We perceive this insalivating and permeating activity with our sense of taste. During insalivation we taste the food. Just as we perceive colours with the eyes, so we perceive the flavour of food with the sense of taste.

So, what we eat is insalivated and tasted, savoured, in the mouth. Through our sense of taste we become aware of what we eat. The insalivating process prepares the food for further processing and absorption by the body. But in order to achieve this, the saliva must contain a certain substance called ptyalin, which is produced by the salivary glands and transforms our food so that the stomach can then process it further.

Once our food has been insalivated and permeated with ptyalin, it enters the stomach through the oesophagus. There the food has to be processed further, and for this another special substance is required. This substance is produced in the stomach, just as saliva and the ptyalin it contains are secreted in the mouth. Our stomach, then, produces another kind of saliva that permeates our food. The special substance contained in this saliva is called pepsin.

You see, after the age of seven we no longer have any sense of taste in our stomach. But infants can taste their food there just as adults taste theirs in the mouth. In order to truly understand the human being, we must study the infant's soul life. Adults can at most get an inkling of what it is like to taste in the stomach when this organ is upset and moves the food upwards instead of moving it down into the intestines. Then they get an idea that taste can be perceived in the stomach. I assume that at least some of you have had this experience that food that had already been in the stomach then comes back into the mouth. You will remember that it really tastes much worse than everything we eat, or at least most of it anyway. Foods tasting like what comes back up from the stomach would certainly not be considered a delicacy.

Now this unpleasant taste must have originated some-where. Well, it started in the stomach. In our mouth the food is liquefied and then merely permeated with ptyalin. In the stomach it is further saturated with pepsin, and that is why it now has a different flavour.

There's more to our sense of taste than is immediately apparent. Let's assume you are very sensitive and drink some water. Unless the water has been spoiled, it will not taste bad at all. But if you have eaten a lot of sugar right before that, your tongue is attuned to that flavour, and the water will taste sour. You can see that our sense of taste is quite a complicated thing. However, taste as we adults know it does not originate in the mouth, but in the stomach. Children feel but don't think yet, and that is why they don't know what tasting with the mouth is like. Therefore infants must be given food that does not taste too bad in the stomach. Mother's milk, or also milk in general, is such a food, simply because it does not have a bad flavour in the stomach and because there is a kinship between babies and mother's milk. After all, children are born out of the same body that produces the milk. Because of this relationship between the milk and the baby, the milk does not taste bad in the child's stomach, but if we were to feed infants other food too early they would find those foods repulsive. As adults we don't object to those foods any more because our sense of taste has become coarse. To infants such foods would be repulsive because they have no kinship with them. Thus next to 'stomach' I can write 'child's sense of taste' [*see list on page 87*].

To return to the food substances in the stomach, once they have been permeated with pepsin, they enter the duodenum, the small and the large intestine and so forth. If the chyme simply stayed in the intestines without further processing, it would become hard and destroy us. So something else has to occur, a new activity proceeding from yet another gland. As you know, we have glands in our mouth and in our stomach, and we also have a large one behind the stomach. It is called the pancreas. It secretes a kind of saliva that flows through delicate vessels into the intestines. There the chyme is permeated by this third liquid.

The substance produced by the pancreas is actually

transformed in us. At first it closely resembles the pepsin produced in the stomach. On its way towards the intestines, however, it changes. It becomes more strong and pungent, for at this point the chyme must be worked on more strongly than before. This pungent liquid secreted by the pancreas is called trypsin. In other words, the pancreas produces a liquid that becomes trypsin, an acrid substance, in the intestines. It is the third liquid permeating the chyme.

As I said last time, our head-centred consciousness no longer perceives the processes the chyme undergoes. Instead they are perceived, tasted or felt by the liver and thought by the kidneys. The liver and the kidneys have soul qualities and are able to perceive just as we perceive with the sense organs in our head. We are not aware of the liver's and the kidneys' perceptions except, as I said, in dreams; then these perceptions are expressed in a pictorial way. For instance, the chyme advances through the winding intestines and is permeated with trypsin. This acts as a stimulus and can trigger dreams of snakes. At a soul level the perceptions of the liver are thus transformed into something vague and unclear.

So, the liver perceives the processes involving ptyalin, pepsin and trypsin. I'm sorry, but I have to use these dreadful terms scientists unfortunately have coined. Today's so-called experts resent all attempts to clarify things, and they would really be shocked if we gave new names to these substances. We could do this, of course, but I will refrain from shocking scientists unnecessarily with new terms and go on using the old names ptyalin, pepsin and trypsin. The chyme is insalivated three times by three different liquids. These activities are connected to liver perceptions [*see list below*].

Now, gentlemen, let's try to understand how these liver perceptions take place. As an analogy, think of what happens when you hold a raw onion to your nose. Your eyes water, don't they? If you hold horseradish close to your nose, your eyes fill with tears too. Now why is that? Your eyes water because horseradish and onions work on the tear glands that then excrete bitter tears. The effect of horse-radish and onion on the tear glands is roughly like that of the chyme on the liver. The chyme moving through the intestines causes the liver to secrete a kind of tears, namely, bile. The onion must be perceived, must be felt, if it is to cause the production of tears. Similarly, the liver perceives the chyme and adds the bile it has secreted. This then is the fourth liquid our body produces:

Mouth:	sense of taste — ptyalin
Stomach:	child's sense of taste — pepsin
Pancreas:	liver perception — trypsin
Liver:	bile

After the chyme has been permeated with ptyalin in the mouth, with pepsin in the stomach, and with trypsin through the pancreas, the liver finally adds bile to it. Only at that point does thinking in the kidneys occur.

After having been permeated by four different liquids, the chyme is absorbed through the intestinal walls into the lymph vessels and then into the blood. You see, then, that very complex life processes take place in the human body. All the way from the mouth to its final absorption by the blood, the chyme is constantly being transformed so that it can be digested properly by the stomach as well as by the entire body.

Now, gentlemen, if we tried to duplicate these processes in a laboratory, even if we were very clever professors, we couldn't do it; we wouldn't be able to duplicate the pro-cesses of digestion. We would have to chew the food to permeate it with saliva, then we'd have to saturate it with the liquids produced by stomach, pancreas and liver.

Obviously, we wouldn't be able to do all that in a lab; yet these processes are always going on in us, every day of our life. True, we are quite intelligent, but the processes in our belly show much more intelligence than people usually have. The digestive processes are organized very wisely and are not at all easy to duplicate.

You will have even more respect for these processes when I describe them in detail. What do we usually eat? Well, we eat food made from plants, animals and minerals. So there is a wide variety of substances that enter our mouth and then our stomach and intestines, and all of these substances must be transformed through the various processes of insalivation I described.

For instance, think of potatoes. What do they consist of? They consist mainly of starch. When we eat potatoes, we actually eat starch. It is one of our main foods. Potatoes consist almost entirely of starch and of the liquids permeating it, especially water. Because of its contents and the strong life forces in it, the potato looks the way it does. It is actually living starch, which must be destroyed in digestion as I explained. Starch is also contained in other things, not only in potatoes. In fact, all plants contain starch, and we eat starch when we eat plants.

What else do we eat? Whether we eat food from the plant or the animal kingdom, we also take in protein. We also find it in eggs; there it is in its pure form but already somewhat 'deadened'. So we eat protein, as part of meat or plants. We are always eating protein. It is the second most important food.

In addition to starch and protein, we also eat fat. Although there's more fat in animals than in plants, there are certain plant fats. In order to be properly nourished, we need plant or animal fats. They are our third most important food.

Our fourth major food is salt and other minerals. We

must either eat foods containing sufficient amounts of salt and minerals or put a salt shaker on the table so that we can add salt to our food because our body needs it.

All of these substances end up in the intestines and are transformed there. Well, and what becomes of them? Because the food substances have been well prepared by saliva and the digestive juices in the stomach, they can be insalivated a third time in the intestines; they won't harden there but will be transformed.

Starch:	sugar
Protein:	liquid protein
Fats:	glycerine, fatty acids
Minerals:	minerals

What becomes of starch in digestion? It is transformed into sugar. In other words, when we eat starch, it becomes sugar in the stomach. If we want to have sugar in us and if we could produce enough of it ourselves, we would not need to eat any for the simple reason that we could manufacture it from starch. But although it is in our nature to be able to do a lot of things, we are not omnipotent. Thus we do not produce enough sugar, in some cases far too little. In order to complement what the intestines themselves normally produce, we must add sugar to our food. To sum up, our intestines transform starch into sugar, which is quite an art.

As you know, people prone to digestive problems find that soft-boiled eggs agree with them better than hard ones. Of course, eggs that have started to rot certainly do not agree with us. Protein is good for us, but if it is still alive when it enters our intestines, it would become unusable and fetid in us, too. We can't use it in our intestines in the form it has outside us. The protein must be transformed first; above all it must be dissolved. It won't dissolve if you merely put it in water. It takes more than just water to dissolve protein. In particular it is trypsin, more than any other liquid, that can liquefy protein.

During this transformation, another substance is formed in our body as a result of the activity of the liquid produced by the pancreas. Strangely enough it is alcohol that develops there. Yes, we produce alcohol in our body. So, we don't really need to drink any alcohol because we are constantly manufacturing it in our intestines. It is only when the liver gets too greedy for alcohol and won't be content with perceiving the small amount of it produced in the intestines that people become alcoholics.

Some people have always known about this and used it to argue in favour of drinking wine and beer. They would argue against teetotalers by saying that we cannot possibly abstain totally from alcohol simply because we all produce some of it in our intestines. Well, this certainly doesn't justify becoming a drinker and demanding an excessive amount of alcohol. If we drink too much alcohol, in other words if we give in to the liver's greed for it, our liver will degenerate into proliferous growth.

After all, the liver has to function properly. If it keeps growing, the small glands in it begin to swell, and then the liver can no longer produce bile of the quality needed. Therefore the chyme is no longer properly permeated with bile and enters lymph and blood vessels without having been properly digested. This imbalance then reaches even the heart and affects it. That is why the liver of people who drink too much beer and so on is ill and looks quite different from that of people who rarely drink or who are content with the small amount of alcohol produced in their own intestines, which should essentially be enough anyway.

Liver and heart disorders result from excessive alcohol consumption. That is why a large number of people in Munich have a so-called beer heart.[1] Of course, their liver is also damaged for the same reason. You see, we can understand various malfunctions and diseases by examining what happens to the chyme in our organism, by studying the digestive processes.

So when protein is liquefied, alcohol forms and permeates the protein; this prevents the protein from rotting. As you know, if we want to keep something from deteriorating we put it into spirits; for alcohol acts as a preservative. Thus the organism itself can preserve protein by permeating it with the alcohol it has produced. A very wise arrangement, isn't it?

We could not get the same results if we tried to duplicate these complicated processes that occur within us. For instance, if we want to preserve a human organ or a small organism, we put it into spirits and display it in a scientific exhibit. But the trypsin fulfils this function in a far more delicate and intelligent way in our intestines. It produces alcohol and uses it to permeate the protein.

And what happens to fats? Well, gentlemen, they enter the intestines and are transformed by both trypsin and bile. Two substances develop out of fats. One of them is glycerine. You already know it in its commercial form; we also produce it in our body. In addition to glycerine, various kinds of fatty acids form when fats are transformed in digestion. Only the salts and minerals undergo little change. They are merely dissolved for easier digestion. They remain basically as they were in the food we ate; they remain unchanged [*see list on page 89*].

Thus when we eat, we take in starch, protein, fats, and minerals. Once we have digested them, they have turned into sugar, dissolved liquefied protein, glycerine, fatty acids, and salt and minerals. What happens then to these transformed substances? Remember, they are now different from the ones we ate. Our organism has changed them.

Well, you see, a few centuries ago, there was a doctor in

Switzerland who had an idea about the digestive processes I have described. Yet modern scientists despise him. His name was Paracelsus, and he was a professor in Basel.[2] But people there sent him away because he knew more than they did. Even today he is still scorned. Although he was a very intelligent person, he fell off a cliff and fractured his skull. Had he been what is now called an honourable citizen, for instance a city councillor, people would still honour his memory. But he was a person who knew more than others. So they called him a drunkard and said that was why he fell off the cliff. Well, that's how the world goes. As I said, he knew a lot and always strongly emphasized these transformative forces in us. But during the centuries since his time this has been all but forgotten.

To return to my previous question, what happens to these transformed substances in us? In this respect modern scientists labour under a great delusion. They say that substances such as sugar, liquefied protein, alcohol, glycerine, fatty acids and minerals all enter the blood vessels, through them get into the heart, and are carried from there to the rest of the organism. Let me say here that all of these substances are of course now liquefied, some are more thickish fluids and others less so, and the thickish liquids do indeed enter the blood vessels and from there reach the rest of the body. However, gentlemen, think of what happens when you put sugar into a glass of water and drink it. Of course, the water isn't sweet only at the bottom, where the sugar settles, but all the water tastes sweet. Sugar dissolves in the water. The same is true for salt. This glass of water, which we might compare with the human body, does not need special vessels to distribute the sugar or salt everywhere, because they are absorbed everywhere by the liquid.

I told you some time ago that human beings consist of 90 per cent water, or at least liquids. We are talking of living water here, but water nonetheless. Now, do these transformed substances then really need blood vessels in order to be absorbed by the entire body? Does the sugar produced in our intestines need special vessels to reach all parts of our organism? No, of course not. We human beings consist of so much water for the very purpose of distributing the sugar everywhere.

People used to say that the alcohol a drinker consumes enters the heart by way of the intestines and from there is then distributed throughout the body. Let me assure you, gentlemen, if all this alcohol entered the heart first, the person would not die in a few years, but in a few days instead. In fact, it can be proved that any liquid food we take in doesn't reach the rest of the body by way of the blood vessels, but instead in the same way sugar added to a glass of water is distributed in all of the water.

True, when a healthy person is thirsty and drinks a glass of water, then this water is assimilated and added to the chyme in the intestines as needed and reaches the heart and the rest of the body by way of the blood vessels. However, once the blood vessels and the heart have received enough, no more water is distributed through the vessels, no matter how much we drink. No more water is needed there. If we drink just enough to quench our thirst — say one glass or one and a half — it doesn't do any harm at all. But anything beyond that amount, any excess — say, a third or fourth glass — will lead to excretion of the water in urine. This unnecessary liquid will not, as it were, bother to go through the heart, but since our organism is a column of water and this extra amount is superfluous, it is simply discharged with the urine. Just imagine what happens when people sit in a pub or a bar and have their third or fourth glass of beer. You can see them get up and walk away somewhere! This beer did not take the time to go through the heart first; it left by a shortcut, because, after all, the human organism is essentially liquid.

Thus, we can summarize as follows: the chyme, consisting of sugar, liquid protein, glycerine, fatty acids and minerals, is absorbed directly by the entire organism. Only the more thickish liquids are distributed by means of the blood vessels. That's why minerals can be deposited in our head and other organs; they get there not through the blood vessels, but enter the organs directly.

If we'd always feel the salt and minerals being deposited in our heads, we would suffer from headaches. An excess of salt in the head causes pain there. You've probably heard of migraine, which we've already discussed earlier. Things can be explained on different levels. What is migraine? It is brought about by excessive mineral deposits, particularly of uric acid, in the head. The uric acid is not excreted with the urine, but remains in the head. This is because food was not prepared properly and retained minerals. Migraine is not such a 'refined' illness, after all, even though it mainly afflicts 'refined' people. Migraine is actually a rather indecent illness. Substances that should have been excreted with the urine remain instead in the right part of the head because they were already beginning to deteriorate in the stomach. In other words, whatever works on the left side of the organism affects the right side of the head. I'll explain in a minute why this is so.

How much salt and mineral substances can our organism put up with? Remember, as I said earlier, our head contains brain fluid. It is only because of this brain fluid that our brain is light enough for our organism. As you know, a solid object has a certain heaviness or weight in air, but when we put it into water, its weight is reduced. If this were not so, we would not be able to swim. If the brain were not suspended in fluid, its weight would be about three pounds or 1500 grams. Suspension in brain fluid reduces the weight of the brain to a mere ounce or about 20 grams.

However, accumulating salt deposits increase the weight

again and make the brain too heavy. True, being suspended in fluid decreases the weight of the brain as well as that of the salts deposited there. But now think of the differences between human beings and animals. You see, our head is put on top of the rest of the organism, which thus supports the brain. This is different in animals; there the head lacks this solid support and hangs, as it were, over the front of the body. What are the consequences of this difference? In human beings the slight pressure of the head is absorbed by the body. This pressure is not absorbed in this way in animals, and this is a major difference between humans and animals.

Scientists are always trying to figure out how humans evolved from animals. Well, it's OK to try to understand this, but, really, that's not the way to look at human beings. For example, we can't say that because monkeys have so and so many bones and human beings have the same number, they are basically alike. It doesn't change the fact that even in gorillas or orangutans the head hangs down over the front of the body, no matter how upright they walk. The human head, on the other hand, is supported by the upright body that absorbs the pressure.

Something very remarkable is going on in us there. The minerals we have in us move from the stomach to the head and are deposited there. If there's too much of them, they have to return through the body to be excreted. But something else must also happen to the other substances we have in us after digestion. While they move upwards, they undergo another transformation because the upright body partly offsets gravity. These substances in part become lighter, and in part they become more concentrated, condensed, and then form sediments. As we often find sediments when we try to dissolve something, so here there are sediments or deposits along the way as these substances move from the stomach to the head. Well, the smallest

particles move upwards, and on the way they are transformed by the reduced gravity. What happens to them
now? These substances originating in our food now turn
into a kind of phosphorus. Indeed, the nutrient substances
are not merely moving up into the head, but on the way
some of the sugar, glycerine, and so forth is transformed
into phosphorus.

You see, there are basically two kinds of substances in our
head: salt and other minerals, which are still pretty much as
they were before we ingested them with our food, and
phosphorus, diffused like air, in fact in a dispersion even
finer than that of air. These two, salts and phosphorus, are
what we mainly find in our head. The others are present
merely to keep us alive. But the two most important substances in the human head are salts and phosphorus.

As I'll show you later, it is possible to prove that human
beings cannot think properly if they don't get the salt and
other minerals they need. We need salts and minerals for
our thinking. Adding this point to what we have already
said about thinking, you can see that human beings are very
complicated.

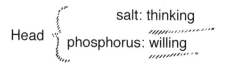

Head
salt: thinking
phosphorus: willing

If we have too much phosphorus in us, which is due to
eating food that's too spicy, then we get fidgety like a
spoiled child, wanting to touch and have everything.
Phosphorus is responsible for our willing. If there's too
much phosphorus, our will becomes fidgety. When this
excessive phosphorus level reaches our head, we will not
only be fidgety and nervous (which is due to the phosphorus, not to the nerves), but we will actually throw fits

and go raving mad. In order to be able to have any will at all, we must have a small amount of phosphorus. But too much of it makes us insane.

Well, imagine someone gives you some salt, and you want to get it to think. How would you do that? But you are actually doing this very thing all the time. In our head we always use salt to think. Next, scrape a bit of fine, powdery phosphorus off the tip of a match and try to set it on fire. This substance is supposed to have will, to be full of will-power. Oh, it'll burn and evaporate all right, but it won't develop any will-power. Yet we are doing this very thing all the time inside our body.

Don't you see now that there's something in you that is more intelligent than your poor head, which cannot trans-form salt into a being of rational thought nor phosphorus into a being of will? This something in us is what we can call the soul-spirit, living and working in us. It uses the salt and minerals in the head for thinking and takes the phosphorus, finely dispersed like smoke, for willing.

If we study things in the right way, we move from the physical to the soul-spiritual realm. But modern scientists don't look beyond the stomach. At most, they know that sugar and other substances develop in the stomach. Then they lose track of how substances are distributed in the body and ignore what happens beyond this point. This is why conventional science doesn't have anything to say about soul-spiritual matters. This limited science must be extended and supplemented. We must not restrict our-selves to the stomach and think of the head as merely tagged on at the top of the body. How salts and phosphorus get up into the head can't be seen. People therefore imagine that the same processes as in the stomach also take place in the head. This is because modern scientists usually know only something about the stomach; yet even there they merely realize that new substances are formed but do not know that the liver perceives and the kidneys think. They don't know this because, after all, they don't know very much about the head either.

That's why conventional science does not even look for anything else, thinking the liver on the autopsy table provides complete information. But the information to be gained from this liver is far from complete, because at the time when it was removed from the body the liver had already lost its soul forces. As long as soul forces are in the organs, the latter can't be removed from the body.

There you can see that a truly serious science has to continue where our modern science stops. That's what's important. That's why we have built the Goetheanum here, to enable scientists to know not just something incomplete about the stomach, but instead to be able to explain the entire body. When they can do that, they will represent true science.

On early earth conditions (Lemuria)

Well, gentlemen, in order to understand the human being even better than we do now, let's look at the earth. We simply cannot study our physical existence in isolation without including the earth.

When you visit museums of natural history, you sometimes find remains of animals and plants that lived here a long time ago. You can imagine that all sorts of things took place before these ancient plants and animals decayed to a certain point. You can understand that at best only the bones of certain animals have remained intact, whereas the muscles, soft tissue, the heart, and the other organs decayed soon after death. However the bones have been preserved because mud and other such material got into them and they eventually became petrified. These petrified bones can be studied and give us an idea of what it was like on earth a long time ago. The earth back then could not have been as it is today because then totally different plants and animals lived on it, and the species we know today could not have developed under the conditions of long ago. Obviously the earth must have looked quite different in the distant past. You'll see that clearly from what I'll tell you about today.

Early last century, around 1810, there lived a natural scientist by the name of Cuvier.[1] It was said that just from looking at a bone he could get an idea of what an animal looked like. When we thoroughly study such petrified bones, even if we have only the bone of the forearm, for example, the ulna, we can picture what the animal must have looked like; for a change in the structure of the whole directly affects the form of each part. Thus we can ascertain what the animal's body as a whole looked like just on the basis of a few bones. Of course, sometimes we can find complete skeletons of animals from the distant past. But even individual bones can give us a good idea of what things were like back then.

I will now describe what the earth was like many thousands of years ago. I'll just tell you about it for now, and later we'll go into more detail. This is what the earth was like at one time.

Imagine the earth — I'll draw a bit of it here — but picture it without the solid mountains we know. Instead, that earth was just like the surface of our earth now after it has rained for several weeks, in fact even muddier. Had we lived at that time, we would have had to swim — and would have got very muddy in the process — or we'd have sunk into the soft mud. Well, back then there were no human beings as we know them. The earth was very muddy and there were all kinds of things in it.

When you go for a walk and collect rocks like the one brought in the other day, or when you go still farther into Switzerland and find even harder ones, imagine that all of those stones at one time were dissolved in the mud of the earth just like salt can be dissolved in water. This was possible because the muddy earth contained various acids that were able to dissolve all sorts of things. In a word, the surface of the earth consisted of a peculiar mud. And above the surface, there wasn't an atmosphere as we know it, consisting only of oxygen and nitrogen, but one that contained all kinds of acids in gaseous form. It contained even sulphuric acid and nitric acid gases. This tells you that human beings as we know them could not have lived there. These gases were not very concentrated, but they were nonetheless in the air, even if only in traces. The air around the earth at that time also had another peculiar characteristic: it was about as hot as you would be if you squeezed

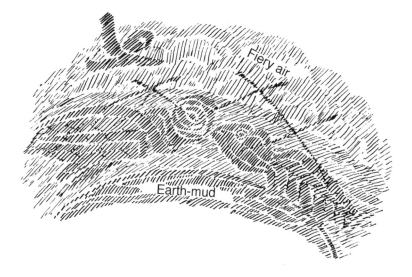

yourselves into an old-fashioned village oven just heated up for baking bread. We would have found that temperature as uncomfortable as the smell of sulphuric acid.

Above this layer of air there was another one; it was even warmer and formed clouds containing sulphuric acid, nitric acid gases and other substances, and it produced bolts of lightning and tremendous claps of thunder. This is what the surroundings of the earth looked like.

To give it a name, let's call this warmer layer 'fiery air'. It was not blazing hot, as modern scientists incorrectly assume. It wasn't warmer than an oven ready for baking. Further down and closer to the earth, the layers got cooler. But let's call this upper layer 'fiery'; what was below we'll call 'earth mud'. Now you have a rough idea of what it was like on the earth back then.

At times the greenish-brown mud down on the earth got as hard and compact as a horse's hoof, and then it dissolved again. Those times of hardening correspond in a way to what we call winter. When the sun was shining in the summer, the mud was liquefied again. And above it was the warm air containing all kinds of substances that later precipitated to the ground as the air purified itself.

This condition later developed into a different one during which peculiar animals lived in the fiery air. Their tails were flat and covered with scales so that these animals were able to fly through the fiery air. Their wings and heads resembled those of bats. When the amount of harmful gases in the fiery air had decreased, these animals flew around up there. They were uniquely equipped for life in this environment. Of course, when the storms were particularly bad and when there were terrible claps of thunder and lightning, they weren't too comfortable either. But when the weather eased up, when there was only a slight crackling and sheet lightning, they liked living in the air. These flying animals were even able to emit something like electricity and to send it down to the earth. If people had been living on the earth at that time, they would have felt the presence of a flock of such birds above them from such electrical emissions. Indeed, those birds were small dragon birds, emitting electricity and living in the fiery air.

You see, these creatures were extremely well and delicately built. They had extraordinarily keen senses. Eagles and vultures, which developed out of these ancient birds after many metamorphoses, retained only the keen sight from their ancestors. But these ancient creatures had senses for everything, particularly in their batlike wings, which were very sensitive, about as sensitive as our eyes. With their wings those birds were able to perceive everything that happened. For instance, when the moon was shining, they flapped their wings simply because they had such a pleasant sensation in them. Just as a happy dog wags its tail, so these birds flapped their wings. They enjoyed the moonlight. Then they would fly around and take special pleasure in creating delicate clouds of fire around themselves, something only fireflies can still do nowadays. So in moonlight they looked like shining clouds. That's what we would have seen in the air if we had lived back then — flocks of shining clouds.

In sunshine, the birds didn't feel like creating such shining clouds around themselves. Instead, they contracted and began to digest the substances they had taken in from the air, substances that had been dissolved in the air. To feed, they absorbed those substances, sucked them in. This 'food' was then digested in the sunshine. Indeed, they were peculiar creatures, those dragon birds living in the fiery air surrounding the earth.

Further down, on the muddy earth, there were animals remarkable for their gigantic size.* They lived on the earth, half swimming and half wading in the mud. A few remains of these huge creatures have been found and can be seen in natural history museums. Those gigantic animals are called ichthyosaurs, literally 'fish lizards'. We can say that the ichthyosaurs actually lived *on* the earth. They looked rather strange; their head was like a dolphin's although their mouth was softer, and their body was like that of a huge yet delicate lizard, covered with very thick scales. They had huge triangular teeth like a crocodile's. They also had fins similar to those of a whale but softer; with these they moved, half swimming and half wading, through the mud.

But the strangest thing about these creatures was that they had huge eyes that emitted light. Well, if you had been alive then, you would have seen electrical dots up in the clouds, particularly during moonlit nights when the shining birds especially liked to fly around. And at dawn, you would have seen a gigantic light coming toward you with a body larger than that of a whale and fins to swim with through the soft mud, fins that stiffened when the creature

---

* At this point there is a gap in the transcript of this lecture.

came upon hardened mud. In some places the mud covering the earth became as hard as a horse's hoof, hard enough for these animals to stand on it. Then they moved by turning their fins into hands that were internally flexible. Thus they could pad across the harder, hornlike and desertlike areas and swim where the mud got softer. If you had travelled then by boat — walking would have been totally impossible — you might have come upon such a gigantic animal, and you could have climbed on it with a ladder. It would have been like mountain-climbing today. You would indeed have encountered a mountain of an animal, so to speak. So you see things were really different back then.

Just as Cuvier could see what an animal must have been like by merely looking at one of its bones, so we can gather from the remains of these ichthyosaurs how they lived. We can see what they were able to do with their giant fins and that they had huge eyes, like a gigantic lantern, that shone from afar so that one could have stepped out of the animals' way.

Further down, deeper in the mud, there lived other animals. They thoroughly enjoyed wading and wallowing in the mud and always looked very dirty, covered with greenish-brown dirt. Occasionally these animals put their huge heads up into the softer mud. However, most of the time they padded around in it, depending on the ground having hardened in some areas. There they usually just lay in the mud like lazy pigs, coming to the surface only occasionally and sticking their heads out of the mud.

As I said, we call the animals with the huge eyes ichthyosaurs; those that lived closer to the earth are called plesiosaurs. The latter also had a whalelike body and a head like a lizard; their eyes were on the sides of the head, while the ichthyosaurs had their huge shining eyes in the front of the head. The plesiosaurs' whalelike body was completely covered with scales. The strange thing about them was that because of their greater laziness and because they usually settled themselves comfortably on the firmer portions of the mud, swimming like huge boats through the mud-soup, these plesiosaurs had four legs, which, though ungainly, helped them walk quite comfortably. The plesiosaurs no longer had fins, unlike the ichthyosaurs who could stiffen and flatten out their fins and use them for support on harder sections of the earth. In contrast, the plesiosaurs had handlike feet. We can also see from their remains that they must have had strong ribs.

This then is the way things were on the ancient earth. The plesiosaurs led a lazy life down in the mud, and the ichthyosaurs swam and flew around — yes, animals with fins could fly just above the ground. Above them, in semi-darkness and in moonlight, hovered the shining clouds of the dragon birds. That's how it was on the earth back then.

As I said, the plesiosaurs were lazy fellows, but they had a reason for that. At that time the earth itself was lazier than it is today. In our time it rotates once every 24 hours. Well, at the time I've been describing, the earth rotated much more slowly, and consequently many things were different then. That the air nowadays is so pure is due to the fact that the earth now rotates once every 24 hours. In other words, the earth has gradually become more diligent.

Judged from our point of view, the dragon birds must have had the most uncomfortable life; they were poorly off. Of course, they didn't see it that way, but had great pleasure and enjoyment in what we would consider a very poor life. You see, there were the ichthyosaurs with their huge shining eyes wading, swimming or flying through the very warm air, and those shining eyes attracted the birds just as light attracts a mosquito. The same thing happens on a small scale when you turn on a light and a mosquito sees it, flies up to it, and gets burned. Well, these birds up there were completely hypnotized by the ichthyosaurs' huge eyes, flung themselves down, and were then eaten by the ichthyosaurs who lived on what whizzed around in the air surrounding them. If you could have walked around on this strange ancient earth, you would have said, 'These gigantic creatures are eating fire!' for that is exactly what it looked like. Huge animals were flying around and eating fire that flew towards them through the air.

At times, the plesiosaurs also stuck their heads up out of the mud, and their eyes shone, too. Thus, when the birds came swooping down, the plesiosaurs got their share too.

All of this makes sense when we put all the facts together for a complete picture. The ichthyosaurs ate most of the fiery birds; the plesiosaurs got only what was left over. And just as the ribs of an undernourished dog show, so the plesiosaurs had protruding ribs. We can still see from their remains that they were malnourished in ancient times.

You are probably thinking that the beautiful birds up there were poorly off. The fact is that they actually experienced pleasure in falling into the jaws of the ichthyosaurs; it was bliss to them. On the other hand, the 'fire-eaters' themselves, although they had to eat, felt almost more uncomfortable than the ones that were being swallowed. The fiery birds blissfully threw themselves into the huge jaws, but the ichthyosaurs began to feel uncomfortable in their stomachs because electricity developed there. After all, the ichthyosaurs consisted almost only of stomach; there was little else in them. As a result of eating this fire and developing electricity, these huge creatures gradually became weaker. Of course, all this took a long time, for these fish creatures could stand even more than human beings of whom we have already said that they can cope with a lot. Over time, little by little, the ichthyosaurs became weaker and weaker. Their eyes shone less brightly and did not attract the birds as much as before. The ichthyosaurs began to suffer more and more from stomach aches. And what was the meaning of this? After all, everything in the world has its meaning.

You see, as the ichthyosaurs were eating and digesting this fire, their stomachs changed to the point of not being stomachs any more. Finally the animals themselves changed and took on different shapes.

Modern science only tells us that there used to be different animals that gradually metamorphosed. This is no better than telling people that once upon a time God descended, took a lump of earth, and formed Adam out of it. We understand the one as well as the other.

But you will understand very well what I am now going to describe. Because the ichthyosaurs and the plesiosaurs ate the dragon birds, their insides changed, and they developed into different animals. A contributing factor to this development was the fact that the earth gradually began to rotate more quickly, not as fast as today, but faster than before, when it had been quite lazy. In addition, the substances that would have been harmful to later creatures precipitated out of the air and united with the earth. This is especially true of all sulphur compounds. Thus the air became more and more pure though not yet as pure as it is now.

In this later state, the air was more watery and permeated with dense water vapours. In a sense, the air had actually been clearer earlier because it was warmer, and the substances it contained were more diffused. Later it cooled off and became very foggy. This fog enveloped the entire earth. Even under the influence of the sun it did not completely lift. Then the mud gradually thickened and what later became rocks began to crystallize. The mud thickened, but it was still there. In some places it was compact, and in between there was still the more liquid, brownish-green mud. And above all this, there was foggy air.

Huge plants developed in this foggy air. The ferns you can now find in the forest are small compared to the huge, fernlike plants that grew many, many thousand years ago. These plants sunk shallow roots into the spongy, muddy earth wherever it had thickened a bit, and they rose up high and literally formed a forest of ferns. By then, the surface of the earth had become a bit more compact and contained various types of stones that were not yet really hard but had the consistency of wax; in between them there was mud everywhere, out of which these gigantic fern trees grew. They developed wherever there were a good number of rocks in the ground, and in between those areas there were empty ones that looked different.

Neither the ichthyosaurs nor the plesiosaurs would have had any use for these big forests. The ground would have been too hard for the plesiosaurs; they would have become even dirtier, for a crust would have formed over their scales. The earth's surface had definitely become too hard for the ichthyosaurs. Both kinds of animals could not survive under these conditions. However, their 'fire eating' had already doomed them to extinction.

If you had returned to this later stage in the earth's development — and 'later' here means thousands and thousands of years later — you would have found it quite changed. Now different animals lived in the mud. Their remains, which have been preserved, allow us to picture what these animals looked like. Essentially, these creatures also consisted of huge stomachs; their head resembled that of a seal but was more plump. While the eyes of the very ancient ichthyosaurs gleamed, the eyes of these later creatures had become black. These animals had four rather clumsy feet that resembled hands, and their bodies were entirely covered with very fine hair.

These creatures led a strange life in this ancient earth. At certain times they were far down in the mud, where they moved about. Mainly they moved their chests, which were huge and were half lungs and half chests. Their lungs were still outside their bodies, as it were. At certain times these creatures swam and waded up to the forests and ate the fern trees. Out of fire eaters, plant eaters had evolved. They were entirely covered with something resembling woman's hair and had huge, plump heads, like those of seals. If you had walked around at that time, you would have seen them breathe under water and move into the forests. With their huge jaws, they ate as much as they could of the gigantic forests. These animals have survived into our time as what we now call seacows.[2]*

Why did these animals develop? They evolved because their predecessors had eaten the air animals, and due to the electrical forces they had absorbed their bodies had changed. The seacows did not evolve directly from the ichthyosaurs, but from animals very similar to them. What these latter animals used to eat determined their outer shape. They were transformed through what they ate.

These details must be added to what modern natural science tells us. You see, long ago the surface of the earth was much softer than it is today. The shapes of the animals I just spoke about developed because of what these creatures took in when they ate the air animals.

Now the dragon birds also had to change their form because the air no longer contained the same substances as before. They gradually moved down closer to the earth and later turned into birds. Down on the earth, animals were always being transformed through what they ate. For instance, the plesiosaurs gradually developed four huge legs like pillars, a gigantic stomach, a plump seal's head, and a tail, but they kept their enormous size. If you step on a small wren, it is of course crushed under your foot. The

---

* At this point there is a gap in the transcript of this lecture.

creature I am describing was so huge that it could have stepped on an ostrich and crushed it. Compared to this ancient creature, the animals living on earth now would have been like mice next to the largest animals we know. Remains of this huge creature, which is called a megatherium, have been found.

The megatheria moved around according to their constitution, that is, slowly, or as fast as their pillar-like legs permitted. They lived on whatever flew out of the air, which had become different, into their huge jaws filled with sharp crocodile's teeth, though not as strong as those of their predecessors. Some of those earlier animals had somehow survived and were crawling around like crocodiles. However, they were usually trampled underfoot and crushed by the megatheria. That's how things were back then.

And only now, after all these things had happened, did the air gradually clear and the water vapours disappear that had blocked the sun's rays like a veil, albeit a very thin one. Now, in this later era, the sun could shine fully upon the earth.

But we must also consider the inner aspect of this entire matter. The animals I described, the ichthyosaurs and plesiosaurs and later the seacows or megatheria, all were fairly unintelligent, except maybe for the ichthyosaurs, which were smarter than the others. However, we can't say that of the dragon birds up in the air; they were acutely sensitive. You may think that we human beings are truly clever, because we would not voluntarily have flown into the ichthyosaurs' jaws as those dragon birds did. However, I don't believe that's true. If you'd been a dragon bird at that time, you would also have done it. Those birds were intelligent; they were very sensitive to the moon and the sun, just as our eyes are. But those birds perceived things with their entire bodies, especially with their wings. Bats, too, have such sensitive wings, though much smaller of course.

Thus, the dragon birds were sensitive to the sun and the moon. As I said, they formed a shining electromagnetic sheath around themselves, and when the moon shone on this fiery air the animals themselves, out of their own forces, began to glow, to shine and shimmer like fireflies. We don't need to overtax our imagination but can deduce scientifically that these creatures had a different sensation of the starry sky than they had of a dark and starless one. They responded to starlight with a very pleasant sensation in their wings, and as a result their wings became speckled.

To a certain extent, we can even prove all these things nowadays if we observe very carefully. Of course, there's not much left of those birds since they had very soft bodies; we hardly even find fossil traces of them. However, close examination of 'softer' fossils, particularly limestone fossils, has revealed wing imprints that can then be studied. Of course, this requires that we open our minds to it, rather than being as narrow-minded as professors often are. Though the dragon birds' wings are gone, of course, we can still find their imprints in limestone. If you look closely at the fossils, you also find traces of all sorts of stars. These are traces of the stars' impression on those wings.

I won't need to add much more before you say that all this sounds very much like what I told you the other day about the liver and the kidneys. We still carry in our bellies an image or replica of the conditions on the ancient earth. These dragon birds were like the eyes of the earth. That means—I can only briefly point this out now at the end of today's talk—that the entire earth was really a creature, a fish, and the gigantic animals moved around on the earth like the white blood cells do in our body. Our bodies in a sense are this earth. Incidentally, the white blood cells look like those ancient animals, only much smaller of course.

In other words, the earth as a whole was a huge fish, a gigantic animal, and the dragon birds were the ever-moving eyes with which the earth looked out into the cosmos. That the earth is dead now is only a later development. Originally it was as alive as we are now here in this lecture hall. The huge creatures I described, the megatheria, sea-cows, plesiosaurs, ichthyosaurs and so on, looked very much like the white corpuscles moving around in our blood, only much larger. The dragon birds in turn behaved very much like our eyes do, except that our eyes don't move around like those birds did.

Thus at one time the earth was a huge, lazy animal that slowly rotated around its axis and looked out into the cosmos with its ever-moving eyes, the dragon birds. What I have described, the fire-eating and so on, all looks very much like processes taking place in our stomach and intestines. On the other hand, the dragon birds look a lot like the opposite of the white blood cells, namely, the brain cells, which extend into the eyes.

In summary, you will understand the earth when you see it as a deceased animal. It was only after the earth had lost her own life that other beings could live here, among them, as I will describe later, human beings.

What happened to the giant creature earth is what would happen if we died and our white blood cells then turned into independent beings. Now we are faced with this huge corpse. It's no wonder that modern geologists, who can study only dead things, examine only this corpse of the earth. Scientists in general study only dead things; they dissect corpses. But if we really want to understand something, we must look at what is living. The earth was once alive and flew lazily through space as a giant creature; it could look out of the eyes it had everywhere, namely, the agile little dragon birds.

All this is of considerable interest, and we will go into more detail next time.

On early earth conditions

We now have to go into more detail on the last subject I raised. Last time I talked about the strange creatures that inhabited the earth and how they lived. I also said that at one stage the earth itself was a living organism, a being.

In various museums we still have remains of ichthyosaurs, plesiosaurs, megatheria and seacows. When we study them, we find that all these animals have one thing in common. Their bodies were enveloped by an armour of scales, and they had strong, heavy forearms or paws. They were so large that you could have taken a walk on them. You could have hit them with a big hammer without really hurting them, because of their protective scale armour. All that is left of these ancient creatures, although in much smaller form, are turtles and crocodiles. Though they are much smaller, these animals are the descendants of those prehistoric creatures, which, as I said, wore an armour of horn plates.

Let us now try to get an idea of how they developed their armour of horn plates. In order to investigate this matter, we have to begin with the smallest details. Imagine that a dog is injured. Animals have remarkable healing instincts, and you have probably noticed what a dog does when it is injured. First of all, it usually licks the wound, insalivates it. Then the dog likes nothing better than lying in the sun and letting the sun shine upon the wound. What happens then? A kind of crust forms over the wound. We can picture it as follows. If the injury is here [*see drawing, over*], the dog will cover the entire wound surface with saliva and then let the sun shine on it. The sun works upon the saliva, and out of

this concoction a hard crust forms under which the wound can heal. Dogs have remarkable healing instincts, out of which they take the right steps for healing themselves.

Now we can enlarge on this. We can observe a strange phenomenon that will help us understand how the dog's wound heals. You know that we inhale air. In the process oxygen enters and spreads throughout our bodies; this enables us to live. Without oxygen we would suffocate immediately. What do we do in return? We are not very grateful to the air that gives us the oxygen. Inside our bodies we combine the oxygen with carbon to form carbon dioxide, which we then exhale. We are actually quite ungrateful to our environment and constantly pollute it. If we were sur-rounded only by carbon dioxide, we would suffocate. The fresh air is transformed inside us; we exhale the product and actually pollute our environment with it. We constantly exhale carbon dioxide, in which no human being or animal could survive. Thus you can see that animal life basically consists of inhaling life-sustaining substances out of the environment and giving back harmful ones in return.

Animal life would soon be in a bad state if all creatures behaved as 'indecently' as human beings and animals, who pollute the air. If all forms of life did the same, the earth would long since have reached a condition where nothing could live any longer, and the entire earth would be nothing but a huge cemetery. It is a good thing that the plants do not behave so indecently, but do the opposite. Whereas we and the animals inhale oxygen and poison the air with the exhaled carbon dioxide, the plants inhale carbon dioxide, retain the carbon and release the oxygen. Due to the existence of plants, especially of forests, life on earth can continue. If there were no forests, or if huge corporations were to cut down the trees, as they already do to some extent, life would become much more unhealthy. It is vital to understand that we need the forests. If we are merely interested in the lumber and cut down the trees, we gradually make life on earth impossible. We can say, then, that the way things stand on earth, human beings and animals actually behave badly because they pollute their environment, whereas plants and forests regenerate it.

You see, gentlemen, this is the way things are now; but they were not always like that. We must realize that the earth has changed and that it was quite different at the time I described a few days ago. If you went for a walk now, you could not come upon icthyosaurs, as you might have at that time. The earth changes constantly and will look different in the future. Yet what can you gather from all we have learned so far? You see that what we have inside ourselves and what we give off cannot sustain us. We must receive something in addition. At this stage in evolution, we must receive what the plants can give us if we are to live. We cannot exist solely on what we have within ourselves. It would destroy us.

You can see very clearly that what is useful and beneficial to us when we have it inside ourselves destroys us when it reaches us from the outside. For example, we would be in a bad state if we had too much oxygen in us. Yet we must constantly get oxygen from the outside. In other words, substances that are harmful when inside us are of benefit when they reach us from the outside, and those that are beneficial when inside us are noxious when they flow into us from the outside. It is very important to understand this.

Now that we have understood that something has to flow

into us that is different from what is inside us, let us return to the past again. In our imagination let us go back to the period when ichthyosaurs were half swimming and half wading all over the earth and when plesiosaurs were hopping around. You will remember what I said about those conditions. But there was also a period prior to this one. What were things like in very ancient times, even before the ichthyosaurs and plesiosaurs?

Well, gentlemen, judging by the remains left by this distant past, the animals of that period were even more clumsy than the later ones. You know, you can study plesiosaurs in museums. You will see their gigantic size, their thick scale armour, heavy like a medieval knight's armour, and their awkward legs. You can imagine that these fellows were not nimble or graceful at all, but terribly clumsy. But with all their physical awkwardness, they still had fin-like feet, which enabled them to swim and to hold on to things. In a way, they were modern creatures compared to the ones before them. Still earlier animals, which preceded the ichthyosaurs, plesiosaurs and megatheria, were even more awkward because they had practically nothing but a soft body that was not very differentiated. There was something like a head up front, a fairly long tail at the back, and around everything an enormous scale armour.

If you have ever seen an oyster, you can think of it as a tiny dwarf compared to these ancient creatures. Its entire body is jellylike, slimy, and surrounded by a shell. If you now picture the shell slightly changed and covered with scales like a turtle's and picture a soft oyster body inside it, you will get an idea of the animals that inhabited the earth prior to the ichthyosaurs and the megatheria.

At that time the earth was of a thickish consistency, thicker than milk. The mountains we know today were still dissolved in it. The earth was a lump of fairly thick sauce in space. In it floated giant oysters, which would have dwarfed this entire hall. They were so enormous that you could have drawn all of France on their backs; all of France would have easily fit there. The older ones of these animals were so huge because the earth as well was still huge.

So, there once lived on the earth gigantic creatures that consisted actually only of a jellylike substance and that could only move the way our oysters do, except that the latter require much thinner water. These jellylike creatures wore a gigantic armour like our turtles and swam around in the thickish liquid of the earth.

You can compare the earth of that period with a huge bowl of thick soup containing dumplings. These you must imagine so solid on one side that you would lose some teeth biting into them and very soft on the other. Just imagine that you could remove the hard portion like a hat. The other part was so soft that you could have eaten it; it was softer than the thick liquid earth in which these creatures were floating.

These ancient animals had something that you can still see today in certain small insects. For instance, you have probably all seen snails crawling along. You can follow their tracks because they leave a trail of slime. Nowadays the sun dries up the slime, and so it does not have much significance. But in those very ancient times, when the earth was not yet completely solid, the animals I described also left such slime behind, which then mixed with the thick earth soup. These creatures were therefore of benefit to the earth.

Nowadays you can observe only traces of such things. For instance, when you walk down a path after a good rainfall, especially around the Goetheanum here, on rainy days earthworms crawl around everywhere. Where are they the rest of the time? They live in the earth, where they make tunnels to crawl through. You see, if it were not for these earthworms, our fields would be far less fertile, for the substances they leave behind change the soil. We should never get the idea that anything in nature is superfluous.

The giant oysters in ancient times did something quite similar; they constantly excreted slime that renewed the liquid earth. But things are a bit different nowadays. No matter how much of these substances our snails and earthworms secrete and add to the earth, their excretions die off in the earth as it is now. We certainly profit from what earthworms and snails leave behind in the soil of fields and meadows; it is an excellent fertilizer when it sinks into the earth. But you see, what these animals give to the earth does not come alive; it does not have life forces.

But in ancient times when the giant oysters excreted substances into the liquid earth, something remarkable took place, something that occurs in a similar form even today. The fertilization process in most lower animals—and even in some more developed ones—is different from fertilization in higher animals and human beings. The females of fish, toads, and other amphibians, deposit a clump of eggs somewhere, and the males then drop their semen on these eggs and fertilize them. The fertilization thus occurs outside the female's body. In other words, the female deposits the eggs somewhere and leaves. The male finds them, fertilizes them, and leaves as well. The fertilization process is fully external and will come to nothing if the sun does not shine upon these fertilized eggs. Without the sun, they will die off. But if the sun shines on the fertilized eggs, they will develop into young animals. This process is still taking place in our time.

At the time when these giant oysters swam around in the earth soup, the slime they excreted made it possible for new huge creatures like this to develop again and again out of the earth. The old ones died, but new ones developed out of the earth. Thus the earth itself gave birth to these very clumsy, gigantic animals and in turn was fertilized by their secretions. You can imagine, then, that at one time the entire earth was a living organism, a living being. Its life had to be sustained through the slime these creatures constantly excreted. If the thick earth soup had existed by itself, these huge animals would soon have died too. They excreted the slime and thus constantly maintained the life of the earth, enabling it in turn to give birth to new creatures, which again fertilized the earth and so forth.

But they would have been unable to excrete the slime if it had not been for something else. I mentioned that the earth was like a thick soup. But the animals' slime was much thinner. How was it possible that the animals had slime of thinner consistency than the earth itself? At first glance we would think that it was impossible for lumps of thin slime to originate in the thickish liquid of the earth.

You see, gentlemen, if you dissolve salt in a glass of water, it may happen that some of it sinks down and forms a deposit at the bottom of the glass. Now the water has become thinner than before, when all the salt was still dissolved in it. The thinner solution is near the top, and the thicker liquid is near the bottom. If you now turned the glass upside down, the entire salt solution would of course run out, and there would be no deposit. But this imaginary reversal illustrates the conditions of the ancient earth. In this thick earth soup lived the huge oysters. They had a scale armour at the top and slime below. What did their shells actually consist of? They were nothing else than deposited earth matter. Just as some salt will precipitate out of the solution and settle at the bottom, so the material for the shells had separated out of the thicker earth substance; however, it moved upwards and formed a deposit there while the thinner matter remained at the bottom. So in a manner of speaking, the reversed glass, or head, could rise out of the water. Only the salt, as it were, rose to the top.

And what happened to this salt? Well, gentlemen, let us

go back to what the dog does when it has a wound. First it licks the wound, and then it lets the sun shine upon it. The fluid on the surface thickens and kills something inside the wound. Otherwise bacteria would enter, enlarge the affected area, and the animal would die. You see, a sort of shell forms here, a crust forms out of materials from inside. The slimelike liquid the dog puts onto the wound comes from its insides. When the sun shines on this liquid, the warmth thickens it.

It was the same with ancient animals. The sun was shining upon this thick earth soup, and as a result certain areas within it thickened in the same way a scab develops upon a dog's wound. These became shells for the oysters. Underneath this thickened mass of the shells the slime was now thinner. This is how the giant oysters came about.

Yet they would not have been there if sun had not been shining upon them. Without sunshine they could not have existed. We thus have the strange phenomenon that in the daytime the sun shone upon the semi-liquid earth, drawing forth these huge oysters.

But when it really comes down to it, it would not have benefited the earth that, while moving through this thick soup, the animals fertilized it by means of the thin slime they excreted. This by itself would not have been sufficient. The earth must have contained something else. It must have been similar to an egg. Only then could it have been properly fertilized. That is understandable, isn't it? Only if the earth had been like an egg could it have been fertilized.

To understand that condition when the earth was a thick soup, we must examine how an egg can be fertilized. We have discussed the male creatures in ancient times, the ones that fertilized the earth. But then the entire earth would have had to be the female counterpart, a huge collective egg. How could that have been possible?

If you wish to understand something like this, you have to observe the world around you closely. You will be surprised, but I have to draw your attention to something else for a moment, to something modern people no longer are fully conscious of. Yet, it is not just because they want to appear mysterious that poets depict lovers walking in moonlight when they want to describe persons in love. The moon has indeed always strongly affected human imagination.

You may think that this has nothing to do with our present topic. But it does. Moonlight activates our imagination. This is something quite remarkable. When the learned people of our time have an occasional burst of intelligence, they come up with some rather nice ideas. For instance, some time ago there was a learned man in Paris who realized that with all the medications we now have we can achieve only very little.[1] It is indeed quite remarkable that a scholar in Paris finally found this out! He thought that in order to improve people's health, one should perhaps do something different. You will be surprised to hear what he said. He advised people to read Goethe's *Faust* very thoroughly.[2] Rather than take in all sorts of things that merely involve the intellect, he said they would be better off reading *Faust* because it stimulates the imagination, which is a good thing. Even such a learned man of the materialist school of thought encouraged people to read Goethe's *Faust*, because it activates the imagination. He said that people nowadays are so clever and use only their intellect. But, he claimed, the intellect actually makes people ill. If they read *Faust* and immerse themselves in all its images, they will be much healthier.

This learned man wanted people to imbue themselves with healthy vitality, with life forces. You see, an insight like that is a unique, light-filled moment, of which modern science does not have very many. Modern science here achieved a healthy understanding, healthy because its application helps us digest better. This is really true: when reading Goethe's *Faust* we digest better than when studying all other learned, academic works. They ruin our digestion, but through *Faust* our stomachs become ever healthier; and so do the other organs. Why is this so? Because this play sprang out of imagination, not out of the intellect.

Just think of this for a moment: whenever people allow themselves to be influenced by the moon, their imagination is activated. More than anything else, the moon stimulates our growth forces, because these two are interrelated. Isn't it true that when we go for a walk in the moonlight, we feel a bit warmed through; in other words, we feel that our growth forces are being stimulated? Of course, nowadays this occurs only to a small extent.

Yet the fact remains that the moon is connected with all aspects of human life. Let me mention a detail here that strongly indicates that the moon is indeed connected with life. Nowadays we are often reminded of things people in earlier times used to know. For example, I told you about the Roman Head of Janus with its two faces; that will give you an idea that people used to know more than we do now. They were not more 'intelligent', but they certainly knew more. Nowadays, when all previous knowledge is buried under our 'intelligence', we say, for example, that the unborn child is carried in the womb for nine months. Well, medicine has not only preserved Latin words, but also some of the old concepts. Although modern doctors do not want to have anything to do with the concepts of the past, some of these ideas are still around. One of them is that the unborn child is carried in the womb for ten months. How can this be, gentlemen? Well, you can figure it out for yourselves: one moon month is approximately 28 days. Ten times 28 is 280 days. You obtain about the same number, namely, 270 days, if you multiply a calendar month of 30 days by nine. In other words, the nine months we have today are equivalent to ten lunar months. Both cover about the same period of time. In the past, the gestation period of the foetus in the womb was calculated in lunar months.

Why was this so, gentlemen? It was like that because people then still knew that the development of the unborn child was connected with the moon. They simply knew, and we can rediscover through anthroposophical research that only because of the moon can the foetus develop as a living being.

But the moon affects only the females of the human and the animal kingdoms, because their constitution makes them susceptible to it. The moon no longer affects the earth, no longer produces eggs there; true enough. And yet, if we study this matter carefully, we find that there is more involved than a delicate stimulus to our imagination and an activation of our growth forces when we go for a walk in moonlight. The moon has such a strong enlivening influence on the bodies of women and female animals that it alone bestows growth forces upon their children or young ones.

But the moon does not enable the earth itself to grow, because too much of our planet is already dead. If it was once possible for the earth to be fertilized, it must then have been much more alive than today. Now remember what I said earlier: whatever exists within us becomes harmful when we take it in from the outside. The moon now shining upon the earth can no longer produce life. Why? Because its light comes from the outside. This is as if the air we had just exhaled tried to get back into our bodies; it could not sustain life within us or enliven us. In our time the moon cannot work any longer on the earth itself; it can affect only the bodies of human beings and animals, because they are protected.

But where must the moon once have been in order to

make of the earth itself a living being? The moon could not have done that while being outside the earth. It must have been inside it! Just as carbon dioxide cannot keep us alive when it is outside our bodies, but must develop in a living way within us, so the light of the moon must at some time have been inside the earth, not outside.

Therefore, you must imagine, gentlemen, that at the time of these giant oysters the moon was not separate from the earth, but dissolved in its thickish soup. It had no clear boundaries and just formed a sphere of slightly thicker material than the rest. Thus it made the earth as a whole into an egg. The moon, which in our time affects only our imagination and the bodies of women and female animals, was at one point part of the earth.

That means that at some time it must have moved away. You see, gentlemen, here we reach a tremendously important moment in the development of the earth. The moon, which in our time is always outside the earth, used to be inside it. Then the earth expelled it, and now the two are separate.

When we study the body of the earth we discover something remarkable. First of all we find that it consists of water in which continents or land masses 'float', just as these gigantic animals once swam in the liquid earth. Europe, Asia and Africa 'float' in water as these huge creatures once floated in the earth soup. When we study the forms of the various land masses, we see that they look different from each other. We also notice from the hollowing out of the earth in various places and from the receding continents that the moon once separated from the earth in the area now called the Pacific. The moon was once inside the earth and then was expelled. It hardened only after it was outside the earth.

Let us return to the old earth condition when it still contained the moon. Then the secretions of the moon gave the earth the function of mother, while the sun produced the 'fatherly' substances in constantly creating those lumps of slime and surrounding them with a thick coat of horn. These floating lumps of slime constantly fertilized what was underneath them in the earth soup, which was kept alive by the moon. The earth, then, was a huge egg, fertilized continuously by the influences of the sun.

Well, gentlemen, if this situation had continued, it would have led to a very uncomfortable condition. The moon would have been cast out; the earth would have become infertile, and everything would have died after all. What happened instead? True, the moon was expelled, and the earth died. But some of the old fertilizing qualities were preserved within the bodies of female humans and animals. Before this expulsion of the moon, there was no birth as we know it now. Just as you take some of the old yeast and put it in the dough if you want to make a new loaf of bread, so some of the old moon substance remained in female bodies so that they could be fertilized. The egg thus fertilized is merely a reproduction of the ancient earth egg. It is no wonder that pregnancy, the length of time the unborn child is carried in the womb, is calculated on the basis of the moon phases; after all, the moon is still involved in reproduction. If you are a baron's son, you must live within the terms of the legacy your father left behind. The same is true for the fertilized egg, which actually derives from the ancient moon soup. It must still live by the moon's terms, because it has inherited its substance from the moon.

In previous times people generally knew more about these things. I will tell you some time why this was so. People used to know more about these matters and said that the sun had masculine qualities. It does actually create the masculine gender of beings. This is revealed in a way in the Latin language, where *sol*, the sun, is masculine, while *luna*, the moon, is feminine. *Sol*, the sun quality, fertilizes *luna*, the feminine element. In German this is reversed, and the word *Sonne* (sun) is feminine and the term *Mond* (moon) is masculine even though in reality the sun represents masculine qualities and the moon feminine ones. Things got mixed up there. If we want to use language in the right way, we should give the word *Sonne* the masculine gender and the term *Mond* the feminine: *der Sonne* and *die Mond*.

Let me conclude today's lecture with a joke drawn from Latin. I want to indicate something here that will become clearer to us the next time. Let us say we first have the moon at the waxing stage [*see drawing above*]. It increases until it reaches the full condition. Then it begins to wane. You see, if you look at the corresponding terms within the Romance languages, for instance in French, which derives from Latin, you could compare the waning moon with a 'C' and the waxing one with a 'D'. And the 'C' brings us to *croître*, which means 'grow'. However, when it resembles a 'C' the moon is waning instead of waxing or growing. The phase in which it resembles a 'D' does not correspond to *décroître* either, because now it is waxing. When we look at the sky, the moon seems to say 'I grow' though in reality it is waning and vice versa. This is how the saying 'The moon tells lies' originated.

But this example has a more profound significance. People were embarrassed to talk about the moon because it is connected with human procreation. This subject gradually turned into something people did not talk about. In the process, they lost the capacity to speak about moon qualities in the proper way. That is why the moon supposedly told lies. When people looked at it, it no longer indicated what they were related to. Doctors gradually dropped the habit of saying that the unborn child is carried in the mother's womb for ten lunar months and instead spoke of nine sun months, which is approximately the same period of time. But in reality this length of time is ten lunar months, not nine sun months. It has to do with the moon and the fact that at one time the earth carried the moon in it, then gave birth to it and cast it out into space.

Basically, what I am telling you is not much different from what some people say about a primeval cosmic nebula, a kind of vapour, from which the earth eventually separated; still later the moon broke away from the earth. But all of this is the result of mechanistic and materialistic thinking! No matter how much substance flows out of a nebula, it could never become alive. You can produce as much steam in a kettle as you wish and then let some substances split off from it and be discharged — it doesn't matter. What I am telling you about, though, is not ancient vapour; what I am talking about leads you back to reality.

Yes, this is reality; not the nebula from which Jupiter and the earth are supposed to have separated, and the earth supposedly expelled the moon when it was still like Jupiter. The real moon is connected with growth, development and even with human reproduction, as I said. Furthermore, the earth at one time had its own reproductive energy and was fertilized by the sun and these huge animals. The moon forces in the earth were fertilized by the sunlight.

You see how we have gradually enlarged our scope in this lecture from the earth to the universe. I realize that I have been making quite some demands on your attention. But on the other hand you'll see that as a result one can learn something of real importance.

The earliest times on earth

Last time I told you how the moon was cast out of the earth and how this affected life on earth. I can imagine that you have many questions, and we will deal with them next Saturday. Today I want to make a few more points, which may raise new questions in your minds as well.

As you will remember, I said that as long as the moon was inside the earth, the reproductive capacities of animals had a certain quality; later, after the moon was thrust out, this changed. While it was enclosed within the earth, the moon provided the motherly, female qualities for the earth. Let me draw this in a general way.

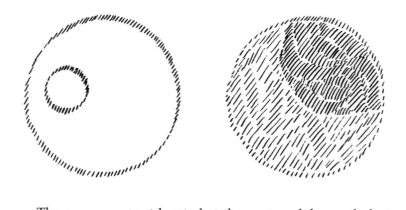

The moon was not located at the centre of the earth, but more to one side [*see drawing on the left*]. If you look at the earth as it is now, you will notice that on one side, where Australia is, there is a lot of water; whereas the part containing Europe and Asia consists mostly of land. In other words, land and water are not evenly distributed, but most of the land is on one side and most of the water on the other [*see right part of drawing on page 128*]. This uneven distribution existed also in the period when the moon was still in the earth; it was lying more to one side, where the earth had the general tendency of being heavy. Of course, on this side where it contained a solid substance, the earth had to be heavy.

At that time the fertilizing process took place in such a way that the moon, contained as it was in the earth, bestowed upon the giant creatures the forces through which they, as it were, supplied reproductive substances. We cannot say that the animals then laid eggs as such. These huge oysters were only lumps of jelly or slime that secreted a portion of their own substance. As I described them in the previous lecture, each of them may originally have been as large as all of France and have had a huge shell, on which you could have walked around. Below this armour there was a slime-like substance on which the moon forces exerted their influences. As a result, a portion of this substance separated and floated by itself in the liquid earth. When the sun shone upon it again (remember the example of the dog), an eggshell of sorts was formed. This caused the slimelike substance of the oyster to expel this portion, and thus a new creature came about. We can say that the female forces came from the moon, which was inside the earth, and the male forces came from the sun, which shone upon our globe from the outside. I am here describing a particular period in evolution, the period when the moon was still inside the earth.

Now imagine the following. In our time, when the moon is outside the earth, it has a different effect than in ancient times; just as carbon dioxide works very differently when it is inside the human body than it does when it is outside, where it is a poison, as I explained last time. If you look at how animals reproduce, you will see that they produce eggs, which must be fertilized. The forces the moon used to provide when it was part of the earth are now in the animals themselves. They bear these moon forces within them. Even when outside the earth, the moon still affects us by bestowing certain forces. I told you last time that poets know this. These forces the moon bestows upon us stimulate our imagination and enliven us inwardly. They do not affect reproduction any more; coming from the outside they cannot work on reproduction, but they affect us nonetheless.

Try to picture now that when the moon was inside the earth and part of it, it directly provided forces for reproduction; now, after the moon has separated from the earth, these forces are implanted in the animals as an inheritance they pass on from one generation to the next. In other words, when you look at animal eggs, you have to realize that they contain lunar forces, impulses that were also at work at the time when the moon was still part of the earth. Nowadays the moon cannot do much more than stimulate the head. In ancient times, however, it primarily affected reproduction. This, you see, is a considerable difference. It makes a big difference whether something is inside the earth or outside.

This peculiar matter of reproduction is essential to our understanding of nature in general since this is how ani-

mals and plants come into being. If there were no reproduction, they would all long since have died out. In order to
understand nature, we must first grasp reproduction.

As I said, this is quite a peculiar matter. Let me give you
an example. Elephants are interesting animals; they cannot
bear offspring until they have reached the age of 15 or 16. In
contrast, look at an oyster, a small, slimy creature. If you
imagine it immensely enlarged, you get an approximate
idea of the ancient creatures I described to you before.
Indeed, we can learn quite a bit from the oyster. It is not like
the elephant, which must wait many years before it can bear
offspring; one oyster alone can produce a million of its kind
in a year. Its reproductive capacity differs drastically from
that of the elephant.

Well, gentlemen, the aphid is another interesting animal.
As you know, it lives on the leaves of trees. We suffer from
its presence, because it is quite harmful to plants. Aphids
are much smaller than elephants; but one aphid can produce billions of descendants in just a few weeks. Whereas
an elephant requires 15 to 16 years before it can reproduce,
the aphid needs only a few weeks to multiply at the rate of
billions.

There are even smaller creatures, called vorticellae. If you
look at them under a microscope, they appear simply as
minute lumps of slime with a threadlike extension along
which they move. They are quite interesting. Although they
consist merely of a small lump of slime, like a small piece of
substance pulled out of an oyster, they can move around.
Within only four days, just one of these vorticellae can
produce 140 trillion others! You could not fit all the zeros of
this figure on the blackboard. The only thing that could
compare with such huge numbers is present-day Russian
currency![1]

As you can see, there is a considerable difference between
the reproductive capacity of an elephant and that of a

minute vorticella, which can produce 140 trillion of its own within a mere four days. Here we have a very significant mystery in nature.

There is quite an interesting French anecdote that appears at first glance unrelated to this matter, but in its inner significance is closely related to it. There once lived an eminent French dramatist by the name of Racine.[2] It took him seven years to write plays like his *Athalie*.[3] At the same time there lived another poet who was terribly proud of himself and said, 'Racine needs seven years to write one play. Well, I produce seven plays in one year!' In consequence, a fable developed that went like this. Once the pig and the lion had an argument. The pig, which was very proud, said to the lion, 'I bear seven young every year; but you, Lion, only manage to have one.' The lion replied, 'True enough. But after all, this one is a lion, whereas your seven are pigs!' This is how Racine intended to reply to his contemporary. He did not wish to tell him to his face that his plays were pigs, but he compared the two nonetheless; for he meant to say, 'Well, you produce seven of your plays every year. But I spend seven years on something like *Athalie*, which is now world-famous.'

Even such a fable says that it is preferable to spend 15 or 16 years on bearing a single young one, as does the elephant, compared to producing 140 trillion within a mere four days. We are often amazed to see how fast rabbits multiply; compared to that, the speed at which vorticellae procreate is actually beyond our grasp.

Let us now find out how it is possible for these one-celled animals to have so many young, when the elephant requires such a long time to reproduce. As I mentioned earlier, the sun is the factor underlying fertilization. Even today it is a necessary part of fertilization. I also said that once celestial bodies are outside the earth, like the moon, they work at most upon the head, but no longer affect the organs of the lower abdomen and the reproductive forces. These forces must now be passed on from one generation to the next. And yet, gentlemen, even today procreation is still in a sense dependent on the moon. In order to explain this, I will once more refer to the sun.

You see, we must ask why it is that the elephant requires 15 or 16 years to bear offspring. You may know that he is a pachyderm. Well, that is the reason. The forces of the sun penetrate his thick skin less than that of the soft aphid, which they permeate completely. This is why the elephant can reproduce its own kind only to a much more limited extent.

You will understand this even better if you think of the giant oysters again. There would never have been even one young oyster if it had all been up to the sun, which shone upon the scale armour, the heavy skin! No, as I told you, the oyster secreted a bit of slime, which the warm rays were able to reach. By drying it off and transforming it, the sun fertilized the oyster and thus helped bring forth a new one. When the sun rays come from the outside, gentlemen, they can produce only shells. How is it possible then that they can nevertheless fertilize?

In order to comprehend this connection, you have to consider something else as well. You may know that after the harvest the farmers dig deep pits into which they pour the new potatoes. Then they cover them up. At the end of winter, they take out the potatoes, their quality preserved. Stored simply in the cellar, they would have gone bad. But in the soil they kept well.

Why is this so? This is a very interesting question, which the farmers themselves usually cannot answer. Well, if you were a potato and were dropped into this pit, except for not having anything to eat, you would feel very comfortable there, because the warmth of the summer sun is preserved there. Towards the end of summer, the forces of the sun gradually extend down into the earth and are stored there. If you dig down in January, the warmth and all the other forces are still down there, five feet below the surface.

This is a remarkable thing. In summer, the sun is up there and gives warmth from outside. In winter, its forces extend a certain distance into the earth, and from there they stream back up again. If you were a potato stored down there, you would feel quite comfortable; you would not have to worry about heating, because, first of all, there would still be the warmth of summer around you and, secondly, the sun forces would radiate up from down below. These potatoes have a good time of it. In a way, they get to enjoy the sun now. In summer, they did not enjoy it much; it even caused them discomfort. If they were creatures with heads, they would have had a headache from the sun. But if they are granted the privilege of being buried in the earth, the potatoes can really luxuriate in the pleasures the sun now provides.

From this you can gather that the sun affects life not only while it is shining directly on something, but also when its forces have been absorbed and retained somewhere.

Now, gentlemen, something peculiar happens. Remember I told you that when a being or substance is outside the earth it has a destructive effect; it is either poisonous like carbon dioxide in our earlier example or it produces scales and hardness like the sun. However, in winter the sun does not work on us from the outside. It works from inside the earth where its forces are stored. There it regenerates also the reproductive forces, which in our time also come from the sun, not from direct radiation but from what is reflected by the earth during winter.

This is very interesting. Similarly, if we inhale carbon dioxide, it is poisonous. But we need it in the form that is inside the body. Without it we would not have any carbon, and without carbon we would not have any structure in our bodies. We need carbon dioxide inside us, where it is beneficial. But approaching us from the outside, it is poisonous. The sun's rays coming from the outside produce shells in animals. But if the sun's rays are caught and reflected from inside the earth, then they produce life and enable animals to reproduce.

Now, gentlemen, imagine that you are not a potato, but an elephant. You would have a very thick skin, barely allowing any of the sun's warmth to enter your body. Therefore it would take you an awfully long period of time to bear offspring. Now imagine you are an aphid or an oyster. In this case, especially as such a creature of the sea, your lower parts, near the earth, would only be a lump of slime. It is quite different for the elephant. He is completely enveloped in a thick skin, which barely allows the warmth from below to penetrate.

Insects like aphids live close to the soil on plants and have only very thin skins. In spring, they can easily absorb what the earth reflects. Thus their reproductive forces are always quickly replenished. This applies even more to the vorticellae, because they live in water, which stores the sun forces more intensively and helps produce the 140 trillion offspring at the right time of the year. In other words, when the vorticellae have absorbed a sufficient amount of sun forces from the water, they are capable of extremely fast reproduction. In our time, the earth provides its creatures with procreative energy by storing the sun forces inside it throughout the winter.

Let us now look at plants. You know that some plants propagate through so-called cuttings. When these particular plants grow up, you can cut off a twig in the proper way and put this cutting into the soil, where it will grow as a separate plant. Certain plants can propagate this way. How is this possible? They can form independent life out of such pieces of themselves, because their seeds are in the earth in winter. This is indeed a very important aspect for plants. If you want them to grow properly, they must actually remain in the earth throughout the winter, so that they can emerge from it. Of course, there is also summer grain, but we can talk about that some other time. Most plants can grow only when they develop their seeds in the earth. Some bulbs can also grow in water, but that requires special measures. Most plants need to be placed into the earth where they can then develop their growth forces.

What happens when a seed is put into the soil? The tiny grain now has the pleasure of absorbing the forces the sun has radiated into the earth. This is more difficult for animals. Those that live in the soil, such as the earthworms, easily absorb the sun forces there. This is why all animals in the soil or close to it reproduce their own kind very quickly. This is true of worms in general, and particularly of those that unfortunately enter the human intestines. They propagate extremely fast, and we must constantly make great efforts to hold them in check; sometimes this requires nearly all our life forces.

Plants can grow directly out of the soil [see drawing, opposite]. They have roots below, through which they push up. They develop leaves, then blossoms, and finally new seeds. However, as you know very well gentlemen, once a plant develops blossoms, it no longer grows upwards. This is very interesting. Its seed is placed into the soil, from where it develops leaves and blossoms. Then the growing process stops, and the plant quickly produces seeds. If it didn't do that right away, the sun's forces would reach only the petals, which are of course infertile. The plant would develop a huge, beautiful blossom of many colours, but there would be no seed. This is why at this stage the plant hurries to produce seeds while there is time.

You see, the sun has the ability to make plants pretty

when its rays reach them from the outside. Flowers in the fields, for instance, receive their beautiful colours from the rays of the sun shining on them from above. However, just as the sun dries up and compacts part of the oyster into the shell, so it would eventually dry up and destroy the plants.

You can see this effect of the sun everywhere on earth, especially in the hot regions near the Equator. There you will come upon birds of marvellous colours flying around. They are pretty because of the sun in the sky. Their feathers are all beautifully coloured, yet completely devoid of life forces. More than anywhere else, the life forces have withered away in the feathers.

The same thing holds true for plants. While they grow out of the soil, they overflow with vitality, which gradually fades away. Finally, they must gather up all of their remaining energy and focus it on the seeds. You see, the sun produces beautiful leaves and colourful blossoms, but in the process it destroys the plants. The pretty blossoms do not contain any reproductive energy whatsoever.

What do plants do when you put their seeds into the earth? They do not simply cuddle into the sun-warmed soil, but extend their growth forces to the leaves; they extend them upwards. These green portions are developed by sun forces, by warmth, light, and so forth. This is how the sun-forces the plants get from their seeds move upwards. The sun-forces reaching plants from the outside, however, will destroy them in the process of creating very beautiful blossoms. The seeds have their vitality from last year's sun warmth, which was stored in them all winter long. The seeds do not come from this year's sun; that is an illusion. This year's sun creates the beautiful blossoms. But the seeds contain last year's sun forces, which were poured into the earth and which sustain the entire growth of the plant.

This would not be quite so easy for animals, which depend more on the sun's warmth reaching them from the outside, from the earth, and renewing them. This is because animals do not absorb the sun forces as directly as plants do; the latter, as we have seen, also bear in their bodies and their seeds the sun's warmth from the previous summer, warmth that had been stored in the earth.

This is a marvellously interesting phenomenon. If we look at it in the right way, we can say that plants and animals can procreate only through the effects of the sun. Yet the sun up there in the sky, away from the earth, is the very factor that destroys the reproductive capacity. This is just like the case of carbon dioxide. If we inhale it, it will kill us. But if we carry it inside us, it will enliven us. When the earth absorbs the sun's rays shining in from the outside, plants and animals are destroyed. However, when the earth can reflect back the stored sun-forces to its plants and animals from the inside, they are enlivened and stimulated to procreate. We can see this in plants; they produce seeds capable of reproduction only out of the sun-forces stored since the previous summer. The forces that make the new plant beautiful come from this year's sun. This is generally true: inner qualities grow out of the past, but beauty is created by the present.

Well, gentlemen, as a pachyderm, a thick-skinned animal, the elephant would benefit very little from the bit of warmth and sun energy the earth reflects back. These forces barely penetrate its skin. It had to store them, as it were, in its own seed from times long past. Yes, the elephant stored moon forces, which it requires for the female aspect of procreation. The moon is now separate from the earth and the animals bear its forces inside them.

A person who disagrees with this could of course call me a stupid fellow to claim that ancient moon forces are still involved in reproduction and live in the reproductive cells, and that the procreative impulses of today originate from these old forces. As a reply, I would simply ask this person whether he had never encountered anything presently alive that contained characteristics originating in the past. I would show him a boy who was the spitting image of his father. Even if his dad had since passed away, I might come across someone who knew the man when he himself was only a boy, and who would confirm that this boy looked just like his father did 30 or 40 years ago. The forces of the past are always contained in what lives in the present. This holds true also for the forces of reproduction. Whatever lives in the present originated in the past.

You know that many people would consider you completely superstitious if you thought that the moon affects the weather. Well, this belief does contain a lot of superstition. However, once there were two scientists at the University of Leipzig in Germany. One of them, by the name of Fechner, thought that this superstition about the moon's effect on weather might contain a grain of truth.[4] So he recorded what the weather was like during the full moon phase and during new moon. He soon noticed a difference. It rained more during full moon than during the new moon phase. He found this out. This does not mean that you have to believe it. Such records are not very convincing. True science must proceed with far more accuracy. This man said, however, that someone should continue his research in order to find out whether the moon did affect the weather after all.

At the same university there was another scientist by the name of Schleiden, who considered himself far more intelligent than his colleague who thought the moon might affect the weather.[5] 'For heaven's sake', Schleiden said, this is ridiculous. 'We must counter this nonsense with all our might!' Fechner replied, 'Very well, this argument could go on between the two of us for a long time. But our wives can help out too.'

You see, this happened back in the old days when the wives of university professors still followed an ancient custom and put tubs outside to collect rain water for washing their laundry because people did not yet have running water back then. 'Well,' Professor Fechner said, 'let our wives settle this dispute. Your wife can put her tubs out during new moon and mine will do so during full moon.' Of course, he believed his wife would get a lot more water.

But the wives did not go along with this. They did not wish to have anything to do with their husbands' science. They could not be convinced at all. Despite the weight of science her husband represented, Frau Schleiden did not accept his viewpoint and did not say, 'I can collect just as much rain water during new moon as during full moon.' Regardless of how much her husband attacked Fechner, she too wanted to put her tubs out during full moon.

Still, this does not prove anything. Yet it is remarkable that even today the ocean tides are connected with sun and moon. We can definitely say that in one phase of the moon they are different than in another. There are some connections. But this has nothing to do with the idea that moonlight falls on the ocean somewhere and thus causes certain tides.

When the moon was still inside the earth, it developed its various forces and brought about the tides. Up to this day, the earth has kept the remnants of those forces that rhythmically vary the water level in the oceans, and has carried out the variation by itself. To believe that the moon is still responsible for the tides today is superstition. But at an earlier time, when the earth was still affected by everything and when the moon was still inside it, then the tides were dependent on the moon. The earth still lives in this ancient rhythm even though it is now independent of it. Thus the earth maintains an apparent dependence on the moon. Similarly, when I look at my watch and see that it is ten o'clock, I cannot say that the watch itself throws me out of this hall. In other words, the phases of the moon still coincide with the tides because at one time they were dependent upon each other; this interdependence no longer exists, but their rhythm has been maintained unchanged by the earth.

We can say the same thing about the reproductive forces as far as they are dependent upon the moon, which means as far as they represent the female aspect of procreation. It also applies to the reproductive forces dependent on the sun, that is, on the sun forces inside the earth.

All animals that reproduce at a fast rate make use of the sun forces stored in the earth and are less developed. More highly developed animals and also human beings bear the procreative forces inside them, protecting and shielding these forces within them. A certain amount of sun energy still reaches these forces and renews them continuously; otherwise they would no longer be there. But these beings would not receive enough procreative forces out of the sun forces stored inside the earth.

Plants have access to these forces, because they carry up inside them what was stored in the earth through the winter until the following summer. The procreative forces of the previous year are therefore available to plants.

But this is not true for the elephant. Its procreative forces stem from a time millions of years back; they are in its seed and have been transmitted from elephant father to elephant son. The elephant carries these forces in its body. Plants are filled with procreative forces generated in the previous year, but the elephant bears in itself forces that are millions of years old. Plants and lower animals can still use the forces recently stored in the earth, which are enormously strong; those animals that depend on keeping very old procreative forces inside themselves, however, can reproduce their own kind only in a limited way.

Let us now return once more to the time of the huge oysters. As soon as such a creature had succeeded in catching the light of the sun, it lost its inner forces and could only use those that rose up from the earth. These the oyster could absorb because its underside was soft. These huge oysters, which were as big as France, absorbed the sun forces that were reflected upwards out of the earth. After these creatures had metamorphosed to megatheria and ichthyosaurs, their undersides were no longer soft. Now the sun shone upon them from nearly all directions, and they had to depend upon the procreative forces they had inside them. The sun did no more than quicken these forces.

Well, gentlemen, what kind of conditions must have prevailed at a very early time to endow animals with procreative forces they could not have received in a later time when the sun's rays reached them only from the outside? There must have been a time when the sun was contained in the earth, when the earth contained more than the bit of sun forces it now preserves through the winter, for example for the potatoes. Indeed, there was a time when the entire sun was inside the earth.

Now you may object that according to physicists the sun

is so terribly hot that, had it been inside the earth, it would have burned everything. Well, gentlemen, you know this only from physicists, who would be greatly astonished if they could see what the sun really looks like. If they were to construct a balloon and travel up there, they would not find the sun so very hot. They would find it filled with life forces. The heat develops when the sun's rays move through air and other matter. When the sun was still inside the earth, it was filled with life forces. Then it bestowed upon the earth not only the limited amount of life forces it provides today, but it could supply plants and animals with an abundance of these forces. At that time the ancient oysters did not grow shells, but consisted merely of slime.

Try to picture sun and moon both contained in the earth and oysters that had no shells, but were slime. When lumps of this substance separated off, new oysters developed, and so forth. They were so huge and lay right next to each other so that you could not have told them apart. What did the earth look like at that time? It looked like our brain, whose cells also lie next to each other. The only difference is that these cells die off, whereas at that very ancient time the huge oyster cells were one next to the other, and the sun constantly developed forces, because it was inside the earth.

Yes, gentlemen, the earth was here [*see drawing below*], and there was a giant oyster, another one next to it, and

many such huge lumps of slime, which continuously propagated. Even in our time oysters multiply at such a fast rate that within a short period of time they can have a million offspring. The oysters in those ancient days procreated even faster. Hardly had an oyster developed than it had its offspring, which in turn did the same and so on. The older ones had to dissolve eventually.

If you had looked at the earth from the outside, you would have seen that the huge mass of the earth resembled a gigantic brain, only softer and slimier than our brains. You could have observed one of the gigantic oysters reproducing its kind very quickly; and, of course, each offspring in turn could produce a million of its own descendants in a very short time. Clearly the oysters had to defend themselves against each other, because they were all so close together. As a curious onlooker, watching from another planet, you would have noticed a huge body in space, a body filled with life. It not only consisted of millions of interlaced soft oysters, but these also reproduced constantly. What would you have seen in fact? You would have seen the same thing — on a gigantic scale, mind you — that you see when you look at the tiny fertilized egg cell out of which human beings develop. There you see the same process in miniature. These minute, one-celled slime vesicles also reproduce rapidly. Otherwise the human foetus would not be able to grow to its proper size in the first few weeks after conception. The cells are so small that they must reproduce rapidly. If you had looked at the earth at that ancient time, it would have resembled a gigantic creature that contained within it the forces of the sun and of the moon.

You see, now I have shown you how we can go back in our imagination to the time when the earth, sun, and moon still formed *one* body. Well, gentlemen, this does after all differ not much from what conventional science says. You may have studied *Faust* or intend to do so.[6] When Faust explains his idea of religion to 16-year-old Gretchen, she says: 'This is about the same as what the priest told me, just a bit different.' Well, gentlemen, you could say that my explanation is about the same as what the scientists say, just a bit different. In their opinion it was the sun that formed one body with the earth and the moon. According to them, the sun was huge, and as it rotated, the earth split off from it. As the earth in turn rotated on its axis, the moon split off from it. Basically, the scientists also say that the three formed one single body at one time.

Then of course some people say that they can prove this; in fact, they demonstrate it to school children. This whole 'experiment' always goes down very well. You take a piece of slightly stiff paper, cut out a small circle, and then pierce it with a pin. Next you shake a tiny drop of oil into some water, where it will float. Then you put the paper circle with the pin in it into the water and move the pin down so that the round piece of paper centres upon the drop of oil in the water. When you spin the pin by its head, tiny drops of oil will split off from the original one and rotate on their own.

There you are, the scientists say, 'Can't you see it? This is what once took place in the world. There was once a huge ball of gas in space. It used to rotate, to move around its axis. And then its outer parts split off in the same way as these drops of oil did. This means that our earth split off from the sun.' You can demonstrate such proofs in schools, because children tend to believe in authority and will say, 'Yes, this was quite a natural process. There was once a huge ball of gas. When it rotated, the planets split off. We saw for ourselves how the droplets of oil separated from the large drop.'

But you should ask the children if they saw the teacher twist the head of the pin. You must also imagine a giant teacher who rotated the ancient ball of gas because without him the planets could not have split off! Medieval artists drew this giant schoolmaster; he was the Lord and wore a long beard. He was the giant schoolmaster who has since been forgotten.

The scientists' explanation assumes a huge rotating ball of gas, but it could rotate only with the help of a cosmic schoolmaster, as it were. This is not an acceptable explanation. However, gentlemen, the idea that sun and moon were once connected with the earth and that this entity moved by itself, was capable of rotating by itself — that idea is an acceptable explanation. A ball of gas cannot move by itself. But the entity I described could move by itself and required no cosmic schoolmaster because it was filled with life.

Like a seed today, the earth was once a living organism and contained sun and moon in it. Both of these then separated from the earth and left their legacy behind inside the earth. Because of that the procreative forces that once came directly from the sun continued to exist, protected inside the female and male bodies of human beings, and are transmitted from generation to generation. And the animals that develop semen and eggs bear inside them the ancient sun forces, a legacy from a time when the earth still held the sun and moon inside it.

You see, this is a real explanation. Only on this basis can we come to a real understanding of the world. Thus we can see that there was once a time in which both sun and moon split off from the earth. We will discuss this matter again. It may still appear a bit difficult to you, but I am certain that you will be able to understand it.

Adam Kadmon in Lemuria

Question: I was surprised to hear that the sun was once inside the earth, which I had never heard before. As I understand the previous lectures, the earth was just like a human being, and the various animals evolved out of the earth. How can we explain the contrasting idea that the human being evolved from the apes?

Rudolf Steiner: I am very glad you asked this question, because by answering it we can move ahead quite a bit.

What do you discover if you study the human head as it is in our time? First of all, you find that it is enveloped by a fairly hard, bony shell. Well, gentlemen, if you look at this shell, which is thin in proportion to the entire head, and compare it, for instance, with the Jura Mountains, you come upon a remarkable similarity. The substances forming the skull are very similar to the lime deposits in these mountains.

You find such deposits mainly on the surface of the earth; naturally they are not good for growing fruit. For that you have to choose areas where fairly good soil has accumulated on top of this limestone.

Gentlemen, you will have realized by now that if you speak of nature you have to include all of its aspects. You know, for instance, that the human head is also covered with skin, which flakes off. The calciferous skull is covered with skin that has a lot in common with the soil of the fields. Out of the scalp hair grows that is in turn similar to the plants that grow in the fields. If we draw a rough sketch of the two situations, we can say that certain regions of the earth contain lime deposits. These are covered with soil out of which plants grow. On the other hand, human beings have calciferous skulls that are covered with the scalp, and out of this skin our hair grows. In other words, I can draw both the surface of the earth and that of the human head in a similar way.

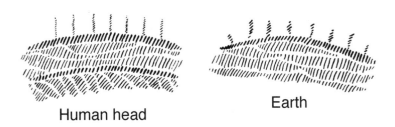

Human head   Earth

Now you may remember something I mentioned to you before, namely, that farther down in the earth we find the remains of ancient plants and animals. Remember, I described them to you. For instance, the ichthyosaurs and plesiosaurs were fairly large creatures. And when we look inside the human head what did I tell you we find there? I said that our blood has white corpuscles swimming in it; in a way they are small creatures, too. In our heads, these microscopic organisms are constantly being revived during the night, but are otherwise always on the point of dying off; they are, as it were, half dead. When we study the human organism, we find a lessening of life forces the closer we come to the head. For instance, the skin between the brain and skull is almost totally lifeless. Thus when we look inside the head, we find dying matter.

You know, don't you, that scientists nowadays are not so keen on dealing with living human beings, but prefer examining corpses on the autopsy table? Well, when they examine the head of a deceased person, they will indeed come upon the hard shell and beneath it the lifeless brain cells, which are actually fossilized blood cells. Thus the human head greatly resembles the surface of the earth.

Once we have penetrated this hard, lifeless skin and reached the brain, we find in it fossilization everywhere, just as we do upon the surface of the earth. In other words, our planet resembles the head of a deceased human being. Since the earth is much larger, everything appears different at first glance; but after close study, we must say that the earth is a huge human head, indeed, a huge, dead human head.

Well, gentlemen, of course, something can't have died if it has never been alive in the first place. Impossible, isn't it? Only conventional science makes such a claim. I am certain, however, that you would consider yourselves quite stupid if you found a lifeless human head somewhere and said, 'This head formed itself out of some substances.' You would never make such a statement but would say instead, 'Something that looks like this must at one time have belonged to a living human being, must have been filled with life.' In other words, if a person equipped with common sense studies the earth today and comes upon a lifeless human head, he must, unless he is stupid, conclude that this was once alive, that the earth was at one time like a living human head and lived in the universe as we live on the earth today.

The human head, of course, cannot live unless it receives blood from the rest of the body, though you may be able to show a human head separate from the body for entertainment. For example, as a young boy I lived in a village, and sometimes touring show-people came and set up a booth. When you walked by, you heard someone shout out, 'Ladies and gentlemen, this way! The next show is about to start. Come and see a live human head that can talk.' Indeed, that was what they showed. As you know, this can be arranged through various mirrors that do not show the body, but only the head.

However, normally the head cannot exist by itself. The rest of the human body must supply it with blood and nourish it in order to keep it alive. The earth, too, must once have been in a condition to get sustenance from the entire cosmos. Well, are there any reasons to maintain that the earth really was something like a human being and able to get its nourishment from the universe?

Many people have pondered the question of how the sun was once connected with the earth. Remember, I explained this to you. The sun and the earth were connected a very long time ago; then the sun split off and began to send light and warmth from outside to the earth. Even the warmth contained in the earth now comes from the sun and is stored throughout the winter. It is possible to calculate how much heat the sun gives off; physicists have done it. The amount is enormous, millions and millions of calories.

However, gentlemen, when they were doing these calculations, the physicists became quite worried. For they found out not only the huge amounts of heat and energy the sun emits every year, but they also realized that if their figures were correct, the sun should long since have cooled off and we should all have frozen to death. The calculations were correctly done, but they did not correspond to the facts. That can happen. We can figure things out, we can calculate something very nicely, but just because the calculation comes out so nicely does not mean that it reveals the truth.

Around the middle of the nineteenth century there lived a physicist in Swabia by the name of Julius Robert Mayer, who had some very interesting thoughts.[1] He worked in Heilbronn, Württemberg, as a physician. Like Darwin, he made interesting discoveries on a voyage around the world. On the islands of southern Asia he discovered that human blood looks different in warm climates than it does in colder regions. These observations led Mayer to interesting facts. He recorded them in a brief essay that he mailed in 1841 to the most distinguished German journal of natural science.[2] The editor returned it, saying that Mayer's points were insignificant, dilettantish, and stupid. In our time those same people, or rather their successors, consider these facts one of the greatest discoveries of the nineteenth century!

The editors of Poggendorff's *Annals of Physics and Chemistry*, Germany's most prominent scientific journal of the time, rejected Mayer's treatise. But that was not all: Mayer was also put into a lunatic asylum! Mind you, his scientific findings were not quite accurate, but he was so enthusiastic about them that he behaved differently from other people — who, after all, did not know what he knew. Well, his colleagues noticed the changes in his behaviour and had him locked up.

We are here speaking of a scientific discovery that came from a person who was put into an asylum on account of his discovery. If you visit the most important town square of Heilbronn in Swabia today, you will find a monument erected there in Mayer's memory. But it was put up after his time. This is merely an example to show how people treat those who think a bit more than they do.

You see, Julius Robert Mayer not only thought about the influence of warmth on blood, but he also pondered the question of how the sun may acquire warmth in the first place. Other scientists merely calculate how much energy the sun emits. But he also asked, 'Where does it all come from?'

What are physicists doing? They follow the same train of thought as those who say about a person, 'He has eaten enough food and is now satisfied. Some of the energy from the food is stored in his body fat and muscle tissue. The person draws on this reserve when there is nothing to eat. Thus he can last up to 40 or even 60 days without food. But then he will die unless he gets food again.' Similarly, physicists calculated how much energy the sun emits every day after having miraculously acquired this warmth. Nobody gave any thought to how the sun had 'eaten its food'; all people did was calculate how much energy it gives off.

Julius Robert Mayer, however, asked this question. He found that every year a certain number of celestial bodies that are like comets fly into the sun. You see, those are the food the sun takes in. Even to this day, when we look up to the sun, we can see that the sun has a healthy appetite; it consumes a large number of comets every year. Just as we eat and thus develop energy, so the sun eats comets, so to speak, and thus develops warmth.

Now, gentlemen, when comets have shattered and fallen down to earth, we find their hard iron cores. But these are only the parts of the comet that fall down. We humans also have iron in our blood. If a person were broken to pieces somewhere like a comet, and only the iron of his body fell down, people would probably say, 'There is something up there that lit up for a time and evidently consists of iron.' Since comets disintegrate into meteorites, which consist of iron, people say that the comets themselves are made of iron. But this is the same nonsense as believing that human beings consist of iron just because they have iron in their blood and a small lump of iron would be all that's left after they disintegrate.

So, we find meteorites; they are the remains of shattered comets. But the comets themselves are something quite different; they are alive! The sun, too, is alive, has a stomach, and not only consumes comets but eats exactly like we do.

Our stomachs also contain iron. If you eat spinach, for instance, you do not notice that it contains iron in a certain form. This is why we advise anaemic persons to eat spinach;

it provides their blood with iron much more safely than feeding them pure iron would, most of which would be excreted again through the intestines.

If the comets consisted merely of iron, and then fell into the sun, you would see how quickly all of it would be excreted again. You would then observe an entirely different process. If what some people say were true and comets consisted only of iron, one would probably have to set up a giant toilet in space! It is of course quite different; only the smallest part of a comet is iron. Yet it is true that the sun consumes them.

Now think back to the time when the sun was inside the earth; back then it did the same thing it is doing now in its separated state. Then, too, it consumed comets. Here you have the reason why the earth, this huge head, was able to exist: the sun provided food for it. As long as the sun was in the earth, the latter was able to get nourishment from the cosmos with the help of the sun, just as we are nourished by the earth via our digestive system.

Yes, the earth was well provided for while the sun was in it. You must of course also visualize at this point that the sun is far larger than our planet so that the sun was actually not inside the earth, but the earth was inside the sun. We must imagine that the sun contained the earth, which in turn had the moon in it [*see drawing below*].

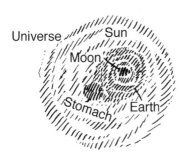

In a certain way, this is the reverse of what things are like in the human being. But actually it only appears that human beings have a small stomach. Such a small stomach by itself could not achieve much. We will discuss the human stomach at another time. For now let me merely say that it has a connection to the world around us. We could say that we actually exist inside the earth, in the same way the earth used to be in the sun. As you see in the drawing, the sun enveloped the earth and had its stomach at the centre. It attracted comets from everywhere and delivered them to the stomach, so that the earth was digesting inside its own body.

Now you may want to say that this is contradicted by the fact that the human head does not do any digestive work by itself. That is quite true. But the situation has changed a bit, and our head does indeed do a bit of digestive work, too. As I explained, the food we eat is first received by our tongue and palate. Here it is insalivated, permeated with ptyalin, and then it moves on into the oesophagus. But not all food substances move on this way, because the human being is basically a column of water, mostly soft with only a few solid parts embedded in it. This means that already in the mouth some of the food substances are absorbed into the head. There is a direct 'food line' from the palate into the head.

You see, substances are not as coarse as we tend to believe. You can realize that by making a few comparisons. For example, you cannot expose a human egg cell to air hoping that it will be hatched that way, but you can do that with a bird's egg. If you expose it to the warmth of the air, it will hatch. Similarly, this holds true for the human head. It would be unable to exist on the small amount of food it receives through the palate alone.

But at one time the earth was structured differently. It had a stomach inside it that was at the same time the mouth, and so the planet nourished itself entirely through this mouth. Thus we can say that as long as the sun was connected to the earth this huge being was capable of nourishing itself from substances out of the universe.

I also told you that when you study the earth in our time, you find that it resembles a lifeless human head. Well, a lifeless human head must have been alive at some time. Consequently, at one time the earth must have been alive. At that time it received nourishment from the sun.

Now, gentlemen, I want to add something else. If you examine the developing embryo in the womb, say two to four weeks after conception, it looks extremely interesting. First of all, you can see the lining of the mother's uterus filled with many blood vessels, which are there only in pregnancy and are connected with other vessels in the body. In other words, this little round form is inserted into the mother's own blood system [*see drawing*]. The blood usually circulates throughout her body, but now in pregnancy it also circulates through the outer parts of this round form.

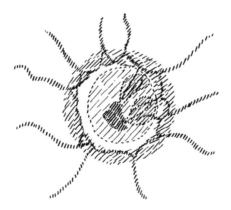

Well, gentlemen, within this form you find all the organs. For instance, there is one that looks like a bag or sac and next to it is another, smaller bag. The above-mentioned blood vessels continue into these sacs. As I said, when the woman is not pregnant, these blood vessels are not there because then the round form as a whole is not there either. But in pregnancy we find those blood vessels, and they continue into the sacs I described. In other words, during the first few weeks of embryonic development the blood vessels reach into this round form, to which the embryo, still very small, is connected. And strangely enough, if I wanted to draw an enlarged picture of what the child will look like in the next phase of embryonic development, I would have to do it like this [*see drawing*]:

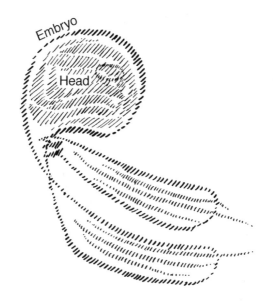

The embryo is nearly all head. Everything else is still very tiny. You see that I drew two extensions to the head. They will later turn into arms. At this point, the legs are practically non-existent. Instead the two sacs I described are attached to the embryo, as you can see in the drawing. Blood vessels lead into them and provide nourishment for the head. There is no stomach nor heart yet. In the first few weeks, the embryo does not have any blood circulation of its own. It is really only head. As it grows into the second and third months, other organs develop and human features emerge. But the foetus is still being nourished from the outside, that is through those sacs; they store the food substances. The blood, however, is provided directly from outside this little growing organism. The foetus cannot breathe yet, but receives oxygen via the mother. At this stage, the foetus is actually a human head; the other organs are not yet of much use to it. Its lungs and stomach do not function yet. It also cannot eat in our sense of the word. All its nourishment must be received in such a way that it sustains the head. The foetus cannot breathe and does not yet have a nose either. The organs are developing, but it cannot use them yet. The foetus in the womb is all head, but, mind you, everything is soft. What will later develop into the brain is here still terribly soft and fully alive.

If you had a gigantic microscope and with this could examine the head of an embryo in the second or third week after conception, except for size the head would resemble the ancient earth at the time when ichthyosaurs and plesiosaurs waded about on it. Where can we find in our time a picture of the earth as it was in ancient times? In the human head before birth, in the head of the human embryo. It presents a clear image of the earth of that period.

The sacs attached to the embryo will be discarded as the so-called afterbirth after they have broken, leaving the child to be born. In other words, what is discarded as afterbirth, consisting of torn blood vessels, nourished the foetus. These two organs, called allantois and amnion, are vital to the foetus during pregnancy because they function as stomach and respiratory organs for the unborn. But as soon as the child is born and can breathe and eat, they are no longer needed and will be discarded as the so-called afterbirth.

If you look at what I have drawn here, you can imagine the following: let us say this is the universe, the earth here, and inside it the human head, and finely diffused all around this we have the sun [*see drawing, page 155*]. Now birth occurs and this earlier condition ends. Sun and moon are both cast out, and the earth is born. Now it must survive on its own.

This process can be described in two ways. First, we can picture what the earth looked like at the time of the ichthyosaurs and plesiosaurs. Or, second, we can develop a picture of the human foetus. It is much smaller, of course, but I would describe it in the same way. We can therefore say that long ago the earth was like the foetus of a huge human being.

It is extremely interesting to note that in earlier times people somehow knew more about the world than later generations did. We will talk more about this some other time. Later generations got their information from a misunderstood Hebrew document, the Old Testament. They pictured that somewhere there was the earth and somewhere there was Paradise, and Adam lived there, standing on the earth as a tiny fellow, but already fully grown. The picture of man they formed out of the misunderstood Old Testament is as wrong as we would be if we said that the human being does not develop from this little thing with the two small allantois and amnion sacs and so forth, but that elsewhere in the mother's womb sits a tiny flea and out of this the human being develops.

This is similar to imagining the earth inhabited by Adam and Eve sitting on it like fleas and mankind somehow appearing later. This picture arose out of a misunderstanding of the Old Testament. Knowledgeable people in earlier times did not speak of Adam, but of Adam Kadmon, someone different. He is the huge head the earth used to be. This image is a natural one. Adam Kadmon did not turn into an earth flea until people became unable to imagine and to believe that a human head can be as big as the earth. They subsequently formed their unnatural, abnormal concepts. They acted as if it were merely for fun that the foetus must spend nine entire months inside the womb before being born.

We must imagine that in reality the human being was once the entire earth, and the earth was then much more alive. Yes, gentlemen, that is how it was. You see, the earth is now a fossilized being just like the human head, which is in a constant process of dying. However, the head of the foetus in the mother's womb is permeated through and through with life. It is in the same condition as the earth was before it became fossilized, as it were.

You see, if people could properly use what science has to offer, they would gain many insights. Science is all right; the only problem is that the people who control and apply it cannot make good use of it. If we look at the surface of our earth, we must say that it looks like a fossilized human head. We actually walk around on something dead that must once have been alive. I have already explained that and will now go on to tell you what this implies.

When I was young, a famous geologist lived in Vienna. In his comprehensive book about 'the face of the earth', he said that when we hike across fields we actually step on fossilized substances that used to be alive. You see, some scientists sense some of the details, but they cannot connect them properly.[3] What I am telling you does not contradict science at all; in fact, you will find it confirmed by science when you study it. However, scientists are unable to make sense of their findings.

So we have found that the earth was once a gigantic human being; that is how it was. Then it died, and today we walk around upon its fossilized body.

Two important questions remain from Mr Burle's question that started us off. One of them is: If we go back in time, we realize that the earth was at one stage a giant human being, but where then do the animals come from? The second question is: Granted, the earth was once a huge human being, but why have human beings become such tiny fleas in comparison?

The first question is actually not difficult to answer; we just have to stick to the facts and not base the answer on all sorts of fantasies.

Let us imagine that a pregnant woman has died and that the condition of her womb is similar to the one I drew for you previously. Now suppose you surgically remove the womb, which contains the afterbirth, normally discarded at birth, and also the embryo. Let us now imagine, gentlemen, that instead of placing these tissues into alcohol, which would preserve them, we let them lie around in a moist area and examine them a while later. What do you think we would find? Well, if we cut the tissues open, we would discover all sorts of minute creatures crawling around in there. The entire head of the embryo that was once alive in the womb is now dead. But because it is dead, all sorts of creatures now crawl around in it. We need only to dissect the tissues to see that.

Well, gentlemen, the earth was once such a human head and then died. Need you be surprised that all sorts of creatures crawled out of it? They still do to this day. If you see it this way, you get an idea of how the animals developed. You can observe the phenomenon to this day.

This was the first question. We will discuss how the individual species developed at another time. But for now you know at least in principle why the animals must be there. We will talk about this in more detail later.

The second question asks why the human being of today is such a dwarf. Well, to answer this, you must once more consider everything you now know. First, you can think about the one human being that once lived in the universe where the earth is now and ask: did he or she not give birth and multiply? We need not go into this question. If this being reproduced, the descendants of that ancient time were called upon to fulfil other functions somewhere else in the universe. This matter is of interest to us only when a certain rate of reproduction was reached.

Well, gentlemen, even in our time you can observe how a small cell multiplies. First there is one. Then it divides into two [*see drawing*]. Each of these two divides again, and the total is now four.

This is the way the entire human body is built. It consists of many individual minute creatures, cells, all of which stem from one single cell. In our blood they are alive, but in our heads they have died off. Thus our earth developed out of a part of the original earth, just as an infant is not born out of an entire other human being, but only out of a part of her. Now we have to ask: why does this not happen any more? Because since the sun separated from it, the earth no longer has the same connection to the universe. Now all these beings remain inside. The sun used to be inside the earth, but later it split off and shone upon these beings from outside. As I said, you must consider everything you now know.

For instance, you know that dogs generally reach a certain size and are seldom smaller than that. Yet it is also possible to breed them so small that they barely exceed the size of large rats. For example, if you give dogs alcohol to drink, they remain small. As you know, the size of creatures depends on influences affecting them. In this case the dogs remain small but become terribly nervous.

True enough, the entire world was not filled with alcohol, but once the sun had split off from the earth the effects of substances changed. Although the human being was initially as large as the earth itself, the tremendous new effects made him smaller. But he was lucky in a way, because when he was still as large as the earth all others born had to move out into the universe. We will hear at some other time what became of them. When the human being became smaller, his descendants were able to remain on the earth and to share it. Instead of only one human being, the whole human race developed.

Yes, gentlemen, it is true that we all descend from one human being! We can understand this, can't we? But this being was not a tiny flea as we are now; he was the earth itself. It was only after the sun had split off that the earth died and the animals crawled out, just as animals still crawl out of dead, decaying tissue. The other thing that occurred was that the reproductive forces remained behind; the only difference was that they were no longer stimulated by the sun from inside the earth but by the sunshine coming from outside. Thus human beings became smaller and could reproduce.

Coming from the outside, the sun's influence keeps human beings small. You can understand this quite easily if you look at what I am sketching here:

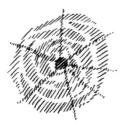

If this is the earth, which I am drawing very small, and if that is the sun, with the earth in it, then we can imagine all forces radiating forth. As the earth moved, the sun moved also because they were after all one [*left part of drawing*]. However, when the sun is outside the earth, things are different. Here is the sun and there the earth, which rotates around the former and is now only partly illuminated [*right part of drawing*]. Now that the sun is separate, the earth receives far less radiation from it. When the sun was still united with the earth, all its forces reached the earth from within. No wonder that now, as the sun rotates, it can shine upon a human being at every point on the earth, but in ancient times, when it had to send out its rays from the centre of the earth, it was able to project its forces upon only one human being. Once the sun began to work out of the periphery, it made human beings smaller.

It is interesting to note that—even though the Old Testament had been misunderstood and misinterpreted for a long time—not only Asian scholars spoke of Adam Kadmon as the human being who was the entire earth, but even the ancestors of modern Central European peoples, such as the Swiss, the Germans, and so forth had legends according to which the earth once was a huge human being, the Giant Ymir. They also believed that the earth was fertilized.

They spoke of the earth as we would of a human being. This manner of speaking was no longer understood in later times because these correct mythical images were later replaced by the incorrect Latin interpretation of the Old Testament. The old Germanic tribes in Europe thought in pictures that came to them like dreams but were far closer to the truth. Those people drew from an ancient science that revealed knowledge through dreamlike images. Later on people misunderstood the Old Testament and spoke of the small individual Adam instead of Adam Kadmon, the entire earth.

Thus we can gain great respect for the ancient, imaginative, albeit dreamlike knowledge. At one time, such knowledge existed, but it was then wiped out. This should not surprise us, for this extinction occurred at a certain time. In Asia Minor, in the Near East, in North Africa, southern Europe, Greece and Italy in the first, second, and third centuries, you could come upon strange statues in the fields everywhere. They were the means by which the illiterate people of those times expressed their beliefs about the past of the earth. In these statues they expressed that the earth was once a living being.

Later other people became very angry and, in just a short time, they simply destroyed these statues, which could have taught us a great deal. The monuments that survived are the least important ones, for in the first few centuries of our era people knew very well which statues were important and had them destroyed. Nonetheless, humanity at one time had a wonderful knowledge of these things, dreamlike though it was.

It is also extremely interesting that instead of thinking as we do today people then were actually dreaming, though they did more of it at night than during the day. Everything we learn of this ancient human wisdom is permeated with the realization that these people observed a lot during the night; for instance, shepherds in the fields observed much during the night.

The ancient Germanic tribes, and others as well, possessed this wisdom of the earth as a giant human being, who existed for quite some time. The human being did not become small all at once but only gradually, until he became what he is now. We will talk about this some more when I get another chance to be with you, gentlemen, because the question with which we started touches upon a lot of subjects.

However, I have to go back to Stuttgart in Germany now.

After my return we can continue these discussions. In the meantime get some good questions ready for me. I will let you know when the next talk will be.

Notes

Text Sources: Rudolf Steiner's lectures were recorded in shorthand by Helene Finkh (1883–1960), a professional stenographer, and then transcribed.

The drawings were done by Leonore Uhlig on the basis of Rudolf Steiner's sketches on the blackboard.

Lecture 1

1   Paul Broca, 1824–1880, French anthropologist and surgeon. Did brain research and in 1861 discovered seat of motor control of speech in the brain.

Lecture 2

1   Translator's note: At that time, duelling was quite common in student circles in Germany and Austria.

Lecture 4

1   Rudolf Steiner, *Towards Social Renewal: Rethinking the Basis of Society* (London: Rudolf Steiner Press, 1999).

Lecture 6

1   Translator's note: The German city of Munich was (and still is) famous for its beer, which is consumed in great quantities by

the population, particularly at the world-famous annual Oktoberfest.

2   Paracelsus, actual name: Philippus Aureolus Theophrastus Bombast von Hohenheim, 1493–1541. German alchemist and physician. First to introduce minerals and metals as medicinal substances. Expelled from the University of Basel for defying traditions, for instance by lecturing in German and criticizing classical writers.

Lecture 7

1   Georges Cuvier, 1769–1832, French naturalist. Considered to be the founder of comparative anatomy and palaeontology.
2   Possibly the walrus — translator's note.

Lecture 8

1   Ilya Ilich Mechnikov, 1845–1916, Russian zoologist and bacteriologist working in Paris.
2   Johann Wolfgang von Goethe, 1749–1832, German poet, dramatist and writer. One of the cultural leaders of his time. *Faust* (1808–32), a drama in verse, is his masterpiece.

Lecture 9

1   Translator's note: Rudolf Steiner here refers to the runaway inflation rate of Russian currency at that time.
2   Jean Racine, 1639–99, French dramatist.
3   *Athalie*, religious tragedy written in 1691 by Jean Racine.
4   Gustav Theodor Fechner, 1801–87, German physicist, philosopher and psychologist. Wrote his book *Schleiden and the Moon* in 1856.
5   Matthias Jakob Schleiden, 1804–81, German botanist.

6 *Faust*, drama in verse by Johann Wolfgang von Goethe (1749–1832). The scene referred to here is in Part I, 'In Martha's Garden'.

Lecture 10

1 Julius Robert von Mayer, 1814–78, German physician and physicist.
2 This first essay entitled 'On the Quantitative and Qualitative Determination of Forces' is little known and was not published until after Mayer's death. It was not actually returned to Mayer by the publisher, but a later essay of his was rejected by the first publisher he contacted and accepted by another one. Mayer's friend Gustav Rumelin confused the two treatises in a biographical essay on Mayer, on which Steiner's comments here are based.
3 Eduard Suess, 1831–1914, Austrian geologist. Wrote *Das Antilitz der Erde* ('The face of the earth'), 1885–1909.

Note Regarding Rudolf Steiner's Lectures

The lectures and addresses contained in this volume have been translated from the German, which is based on stenographic and other recorded texts that were in most cases never seen or revised by the lecturer. Hence, due to human errors in hearing and transcription, they may contain mistakes and faulty passages. Every effort has been made to ensure that this is not the case. Some of the lectures were given to audiences more familiar with anthroposophy; these are the so-called 'private' or 'members' lectures. Other lectures, like the written works, were intended for the general public. The difference between these, as Rudolf Steiner indicates in his *Autobiography*, is twofold. On the one hand, the members' lectures take for granted a background in and commitment to anthroposophy; in the public lectures this was not the case. At the same time, the members' lectures address the concerns and dilemmas of the members, while the public work speaks directly out of Steiner's own understanding of universal needs. Nevertheless, as Rudolf Steiner stresses: 'Nothing was ever said that was not solely the result of my direct experience of the growing content of anthroposophy. There was never any question of concessions to the prejudices and preferences of the members. Whoever reads these privately printed lectures can take them to represent anthroposophy in the fullest sense. Thus it was possible without hesitation—when the complaints in this direction became too persistent—to depart from the custom of circulating this material "For members only". But it must be borne in mind that faulty passages do occur in these reports not revised by myself.' Earlier in the same chapter, he states: 'Had I been able to correct them [the private lectures], the restriction *for members only* would have been unnecessary from the beginning.'

Rudolf Steiner
FROM BEETROOT TO BUDDHISM...
Answers to Questions

Christianity and Islam; Egyptian mummies; astronomy; Tibet and the Dalai Lama; Freemasonry; star wisdom, moon and sun religions; the Mysteries; the Trinity; Moses; Easter; the ancient Indians, Egyptians, Babylonians and Jews; Kant and Schopenhauer, and nationalism.

ISBN 1 85584 062 6; £14.95; 304pp

Rudolf Steiner
FROM COMETS TO COCAINE...
Answers to Questions

Nicotine and alcohol; the causes and timing of illness; pregnancy; vegetarian and meat diets; the human ear, eye and hair colour; influenza, hay fever, haemophilia; planets and metals; mental illness; the ice age; the thyroid gland and hormones; beavers, wasps and bees; the nose, smell and taste; and jaundice, smallpox and rabies.

ISBN 1 85584 088 X; £14.95; 320pp

Rudolf Steiner
FROM ELEPHANTS TO EINSTEIN...
Answers to Questions

Ants and bees; shells and skeletons; animal and plant poisons—arsenic and lead; nutrition—protein and fats, potatoes; the human eye and its colour; fresh and salt water; fish and bird migration; human clothing; opium and alcohol; thinking, and bodily secretions.

ISBN 1 85584 081 2; £10.95; 208pp

Rudolf Steiner
FROM LIMESTONE TO LUCIFER...
Answers to Questions

Technology; the living earth; natural healing powers; colour and sickness; rainbows; whooping cough and pleurisy; seances; sleep and sleeplessness; dreams; reincarnation; life after death; the physical, ether and astral bodies and the 'I'; the two Jesus children; Ahriman and Lucifer; the death, resurrection and ascension of Christ; Dante and Copernicus.

ISBN 1 85584 097 9; £12.95; 256pp

Rudolf Steiner
FROM MAMMOTHS TO MEDIUMS...
Answers to Questions

Dancing and sport; guardian angels; effects of the stars; potatoes, beetroot and radishes; the Druids; Roman Catholic and Masonic rituals; proteins, fats, carbohydrates and salts; Aristotle; nutrition; blood circulation and the heart; honesty and conscience; boredom and opinions; lungs and kidneys; fertilization in plants and humans; light and colour; and breathing.

ISBN 1 85584 078 2; £14.95; 328pp

Rudolf Steiner
FROM SUNSPOTS TO STRAWBERRIES...
Answers to Questions

Lemuria and Atlantis; Chinese and Indian cultures; raw food; vegetarianism; children's nutrition; manure and soil; hardening of the arteries; the sense of smell; planetary influences; weather and its causes; creation of the world; origin of the human being; Saturn, Sun and Moon; Darwinism; earth strata and fossils; Biela's comet; star wisdom; evolution of human culture; lightning, and volcanoes.

ISBN 1 85584 112 6; £12.95; 256pp